Shead, Richard

Music in the
1920s

MUSIC IN THE 1920s

Natalia Makarova in *Les Biches*.

MUSIC IN THE 1920s

Richard Shead

St. Martin's Press   New York

© 1976   Richard Shead

St. Martin's Press, Inc., 175 Fifth Avenue, New York, N.Y. 10010
Printed in Great Britain
Library of Congress Catalog Number: 77–82644
ISBN 0–312–55482–6
First published in the United States of America in 1977

163699

Contents

to Malcolm Clough
affectionately

Preface

Twenty-five years ago many musicians were apt to describe the 1920s as a period of rather foolish frivolity, a frivolity eventually shaken off by the worthier composers of the time, who 'settled down' in the subsequent decade to become, as it were, responsible musical citizens. Hindemith ceased to try to startle his audience and wrote more euphonious pieces such as *Mathis der Maler* and *Nobilissima visione*; Walton, having got *Façade* and *Portsmouth Point* out of his system, achieved melodiousness and maturity with his *Viola Concerto*; even Poulenc, most frivolous of all, developed 'a deeply religious vein' as he grew older. This was the view then held in many quarters. The 1920s were seen as a decade in which wild oats were sown by men who eventually settled down into a steady, serious productivity.

Even in 1950, this picture was not easy for everyone to accept. Were the 1920s really as silly as all that? Kleiber, Klemperer, Walter and Fürtwangler were active in Germany. The Diaghilev Ballet and its rivals continually employed composers and artists of great distinction. At a different level, C. B. Cochran's revues set a standard not since equalled in their area. Among the musical talents which appeared at the time were Paul Hindemith, Ernst Křenek, Kurt Weill, Francis Poulenc, Darius Milhaud, Arthur Honegger, Georges Auric, Henri Sauguet, Vittorio Rieti, George Gershwin, Aaron Copland, Virgil Thomson, William Walton, Constant Lambert, Dmitri Shostakovich, Bohuslav Martinů. More established figures, still creative during the decade, included Richard Strauss, Maurice Ravel, Erik Satie, Albert Roussel, Igor Stravinsky, Serge Prokofiev, Manuel de Falla, Giacomo Puccini, Ottorino Respighi, Ildebrando Pizzetti, Karol Szy-

manowski, Leos Janáček, Béla Bartók. What could the early
1950s offer to match such a roster?

The answer was not a great deal, if one excluded music
from the pens of men whose work had first come before the
public in the 'silly' 1920s.

As the years pass and one grows older it becomes harder
and harder to believe in progress. But musical progress there
has been in the past quarter-century: both in Britain and the
U.S.A. musical life is very much less parochial and prejudiced
than it used to be. One facet of these developments has been
that the 1920s are now regarded in a new light. Weill has been
revived; Satie has been almost over-exposed, at least in the
recording world; much of the music of the decade has re-
entered the repertoire. But much, too, remains to be rediscovered or well understood by the general public.

I have concentrated particularly in what follows on those
aspects of the musical 1920s that seem to me to be most
characteristic of the period. This often means those aspects
which incurred to the greatest degree the strictures of musical
puritans, shocked by what they saw as frivolity, foolish if
French, decadent if German. I have not attempted to deal
with men like Strauss and Puccini, who wrote fine music in
the 1920s, works like *Intermezzo* and *Turandot*, but whose
style and aesthetic had been formed long before and who, in
any case, have now attained classic status. Nor have I made
more than passing reference to the so-called Second Viennese
School, who remained aloof from their surroundings apart
from occasional ill-judged experiments such as *Von Heute auf
Morgen* and an atonal foxtrot or two. I confess that it has given
me considerable pleasure to leave them out, because I persist,
unfashionably, in thinking that the influence of Schönberg and
Webern has been disastrous, and in any case I think that few
have the gift of writing usefully about artistic creations they
dislike. In Ned Rorem's words, 'the twelve-toners behave as if
music should be seen and not heard'.

On the other hand, I have thought it necessary to take into
account the precursors of the movements characteristic of the
1920s, and I have not hesitated, when it seemed interesting
or appropriate to do so, to continue the careers of certain
composers beyond the confines of the decade, nor to note the

appearance of echoes or influences of the 1920s in the work of men who appeared later.

I have tried to consider certain leitmotifs of the 1920s, both technical—the neoclassic movement, the interest in jazz, the popularity of the choral ballet—and more general—enthusiasm for the music-hall and the circus, the fascination exerted in Europe by a mythic America, the *Zeitoper*, the mania for sport, the lure of seaports—as these expressed themselves in music and the theatre arts. Above all, I have tried to show that in their economy, sense of proportion and absence of pomposity the works of which I have written merit the epithet 'classic' far more than some of the ponderous scores written before and since a decade which for liveliness and *joie de vivre* remains unmatched in the twentieth century.

I would like to thank Mr Jeremy Noble for permission to quote part of a review he wrote for the *New Statesman* and Mr Richard Buckle for allowing me to quote from his magazine *Ballet*. I am also grateful to Suhrkamp Verlag and Universal Edition for their cooperation. Finally, my thanks to Mike Humphrey for his beautiful photograph of Natalia Makarova, which appears as frontispiece.

R.S.

1

Precursors

Je suis venu au monde très jeune dans un temps très vieux.

—Erik Satie

The years immediately preceding the outbreak of war in 1914 were a period of overpowering splendour in music and the related arts of opera and ballet. Among composers active then were Strauss, Mahler, Schönberg, Fauré, Debussy, Ravel, Puccini, Mascagni, Elgar, Delius, Rachmaninoff, Stravinsky, Szymanowski, Bartók and Falla. Conspicuous among the tendencies in the music of the period were the pursuit of the colossal (notably in the works of Strauss, Mahler and Schönberg) and the cultivation of extreme refinement of expression (to be observed in the music of Debussy, Ravel and Szymanowski).

By 1918 neither the colossal nor the highly refined had much appeal for young creative musicians. Disillusionment had set in during the four years of bloodshed. Mahler's *Eighth Symphony*, Strauss's *Elektra*, Schönberg's *Gurrelieder*, despite their merits (and it is worth remembering that even twenty-five years ago the first and third were widely considered oddities rather than works of art), were now associated in men's minds with an old order that had been destroyed and that was seen as responsible for the holocaust from which luckier Europeans had just emerged. That this was grossly unfair to Mahler, Strauss and Schönberg goes without saying, and in time the situation righted itself. But Mahler, in any case, was now dead; Schönberg had already changed his style before the struggle began; and of the three composers only Strauss continued to pursue the path on which he had embarked years before. Indeed the opera which he offered to the public in 1919, *Die Frau ohne Schatten*, was his most enormous operatic undertaking and at least a partial vindication of the continuing validity of his personal aesthetic. Of the other great creators of the pre-War era Debussy, like Mahler, was dead; Fauré,

Puccini, Mascagni, Elgar and Delius were soon to die or to become creatively extinct; and the remainder, with the exception of Rachmaninoff, were already writing, or were soon to write, music in a very different style from that which they had adopted before the 1914–18 War.

There was an acute problem for the young composer: the great composers of the period before 1914 had pushed certain musical tendencies as far as seemed possible. It was hard to write music more massive than the *Symphony of a Thousand*, hard to outdo *Elektra* or *Le Sacre du printemps* in sheer brutal physical impact; hardest of all, perhaps (and foolish to boot) to attempt to surpass the *Jeux* of Debussy or the *Trois poèmes de Stéphane Mallarmé* of Ravel in refinement and subtlety. Making, perhaps, something of a virtue of necessity—but also for more positive reasons—many younger composers eschewed the large-scale and the ultra-refined alike and turned for inspiration to such diverse sources as the music-hall, American jazz and the classicism of Bach or the French clavecinists. A good deal of the music which resulted was based on a misunderstanding, total or partial, of the sources of inspiration; this was particularly true, as will be seen, when jazz was the source. But this was of little consequence provided the end-product possessed, as it often did, some distinction, attractiveness or beauty.

The movement away from the large-scale was also a matter of practicality. Stravinsky had been obliged to show the way, for, cut off in Switzerland during the War, and deprived of access to the resources of the Diaghilev Ballet, he had no choice but to write for smaller combinations of instruments than heretofore if he was to have any chance of achieving performance: hence such works as *Le Renard* and *L'Histoire du soldat*. Thus economic and aesthetic considerations pointed in the same direction.

In making this sharp change in musical aesthetic—throwing open the windows, as Dorel Handman has put it—the young could look to certain pioneers, precursors and prophets. Foremost among these, in Germany and France, were the figures of Ferruccio Busoni, Igor Stravinsky, Erik Satie and Jean Cocteau. Mention of Busoni prompts the reflection that the rejection of the past after 1918 was not always as total as some writers have implied. Busoni had been very much a part of the musical life of pre-1914 Europe, both as composer and as piano virtuoso, but his influence on the German musical young was more a matter of prestige, example and precept than of direct musical technique. He had no need to change his style, nor would it have occurred to him to do so: despite the great size of certain of his works, such as the *Piano Concerto*, he had always been basically a classicist. Even Mahler, for that matter, ultra-romantic as he was (viewed from a certain aspect), wrote many of his works with great economy and precision of resources (witness the *Rückert-Lieder* and much of *Das Lied von der Erde*), and not only this technical precision but a certain attitude of mind, perhaps associated with their shared Jewishness, found a powerful echo, long unperceived, in the works of Kurt Weill. But perhaps the most powerful influences on young German composers in the 1920s were the classical masters of German music: Bach, Handel and to some extent even Mozart, though of course the young went infinitely further than their models in the direction of dissonance.

In France the pilots of the young were Cocteau, Stravinsky and Satie: an ill-assorted trio, which offered extremes of worldliness and its opposite. In considering France at that time it must be remembered that many non-French musicians lived in France and took their aesthetic lead from the concepts current in the French capital, while many more, living elsewhere, had studied in France or looked to France for a measure of guidance. This was true of a number of Russian, Italian, Spanish and English composers, and of a whole generation of American musicians, some of them pupils of Nadia Boulanger and thus members of what came to be known ironically as the *Boulangerie*. Thus Parisian thinking affected the work of such different composers as Nabokov, Rieti, Casella, de Falla, Lambert, Copland and Thomson: a far from exhaustive list.

Cocteau, of course, was not a musician, but this did not deter him from promulgating canons of musical taste to which *Les Nouveaux Jeunes* should conform: canons which, to be honest, the musicians who composed the disparate band known as *Les Six* observed when it suited them and disregarded when it did not (and good for them, one might add). Certainly neither Arthur Honegger nor, with any consistency, Darius

Milhaud conformed meekly to the aesthetic 'laws' laid down in *Le Coq et l'arlequin* and elsewhere, and, while the very minor figure of Germaine Tailleferre did so, it was not to her ultimate advantage. Cocteau was particularly associated with Georges Auric and followed him loyally from the neoclassicism of *Les Fâcheux* (1924) to the bloated though not disagreeable romanticism of *Phèdre* (1950) without giving any sign of having perceived an inconsistency in Auric's development. And there is this to be said, that both works, separated by some thirty years in time and aeons of aesthetic difference, do to some degree manifest technical and personal consistencies of touch, such as a very personal use of the orchestral harp. Of course Cocteau's own development as an artist over the same period encompassed many startling changes of manner, from *Orphée* to *Renaud et Armide*, from *Le Sang d'un poète* to *L'Eternel Retour*. Cocteau in his role of arbiter of musical elegance was basically a publicist. Gertrude Stein once said that Ezra Pound was 'a village explainer'; so was Cocteau, but his village was the most sophisticated in the world—his explanations had to be seductive indeed if they were to convince and satisfy that exigent, fickle, bitchy village, *le tout Paris*. However, anyone who could convince such an audience, even momentarily, that Jean Marais was a great actor or Jean Desbordes a great writer would have found little difficulty in drawing their attention to Erik Satie or Francis Poulenc. Stravinsky, of course, needed no endorsement from Cocteau, though he got one all the same. It would be unkind to dwell on Cocteau's pronouncements on Wagner and Debussy. But as self-appointed spokesman and publicity man for Satie and *Les Nouveaux Jeunes* Cocteau had a useful role to play, and one which gained in strength and conviction from his mastery in those areas where he was not explainer but creator, not amateur but supremely professional: verse, the novel, the theatre and eventually the film.

So far as *Les Six* were concerned, then, Cocteau was their 'manager of genius', as Poulenc was to put it later on. But no group, at any rate in France, is complete without a *chef d'école*, and the mantle fell on the not altogether willing shoulders of Erik Satie. Satie, born in 1866, remained until he was well over forty a totally neglected figure. He acquired a little local notice through the efforts of Ravel and other fellow-musicians but he did not become a celebrity until his participation in the notorious ballet *Parade* in 1917. From then onwards, until his death in 1925, he was well-known in Paris at least, though his music was never very popular outside France, at least not until its extraordinary success in recent years. Satie had been a great friend of Debussy, whose music he much admired, but he attacked the 'Debussystes' and publicly stated that there could be no such thing as 'Satistes'. Yet he was an obvious choice as patron for the *Nouveaux Jeunes* since the music he had been writing since the 1880s had all the qualities previously admired idols lacked (it should be added that it lacked many of the qualities they possessed). It was clear-cut, unambitious, brief; it eschewed grandiloquent effects and large orchestras; it relied on line for its effect. As Cocteau said, many years later, Satie 'did not belong to our Group, but his melodic line, so pure, so discreet, so noble, was always an example for us'. Moreover, and this is the astonishing thing, Satie had consistently anticipated musical developments which were to become widespread and fashionable many years later. Lambert wrote rightly that Satie 'had the no doubt gratifying sensation of seeing the times catch up with him'. He anticipated the cult of the music-hall, he anticipated Dada, he anticipated the revival of interest in classical contrapuntal procedures. He was writing in 1899 the kind of music that half the young musicians in France would be writing in the 1920s. He thus became, if not a *chef d'école* in every sense, a father figure, or, better, a kindly, irascible, wise and eccentric uncle to the young.

The difference between Satie and Stravinsky was extremely marked. One contrast lay in their attitudes to their shared profession, an attitude well illustrated by the affair of *Sports et divertissements*. This episode occurred in 1914, when the Paris publishers Lucien Vogel were seeking a composer to write music as accompaniment to a series of drawings by an artist called Charles Martin. Stravinsky asked a fee which the publishers deemed too large; Satie was therefore offered the commission at a much lower fee. He proceeded to take offence at the size of the fee, not because it was too small, but because it was too big. Satie possessed a curious combination of intransigence (he once said 'Il faut être intransigeant jusqu'au bout') and extreme humbleness towards his art. Humbleness was never a feature of Stravinsky's personality and anyone who dealt with him on a professional basis will attest to his willingness, nay eagerness, to collect with all speed any material reward due to him as a result of his creative or performing activities. André Breton's anagram for Salvador Dali's name, 'Avida Dollars', would have fitted the Russian master well enough, and who can blame him?

Stravinsky's prestige in the 1920s was enormous, though his influence was perhaps less direct than has been supposed; but he was certainly a leader, and one whose followers were sometimes prone to stumble. Cocteau, speaking of the role of *Les Six* as 'contradictors', said that they were up against two colossi armed with charm—Debussy and Ravel, and another armed with thunderbolts—Stravinsky. He was thinking in particular of the *Sacre*. Stravinsky would have overwhelmed *Les Six,* Cocteau went on, 'if in time he had not fallen in with our methods and if the influence of Erik Satie had not in fact made itself felt, mysteriously, in his work'. I do not believe that this is true. In seeking 'models' Stravinsky preferred to go further back, to Bach himself, for instance, as did Honegger, Hindemith and Weill. Stravinsky was never particularly keen on deliberately seeking models among other living composers: Webern was safely dead, for instance, before Stravinsky embarked on his final movement towards serial methods of composition.

It should also be mentioned that another composer, respected though not greatly followed by the young of the 1920s, had already pointed the way towards a return to classicism: this was Albert Roussel, whose classical *Divertissement*, Opus 6, for flute, oboe, clarinet, bassoon, horn and piano, had been written and performed as early as 1906.

Finally, the influence of American popular music became very strong in the 1920s. Jazz and ragtime had appeared in Europe before the 1914–18 War (the two terms were used loosely), but serious composers did not begin to investigate them until the War was in progress. Stravinsky, for instance, showed great interest in the albums of jazz which Ernest Ansermet had brought back with him from the U.S., where he had been conducting for the Diaghilev Ballet, though the composer had not at that time heard any jazz played. The results of this interest were soon heard in parts of *L'Histoire du soldat*, the instrumental *Ragtime* and the *Piano Rag-Music*. Round about the same time Darius Milhaud visited Harlem and heard negro jazz played. He too was much struck by what he heard and it was not long before he began to adapt jazz sounds and mannerisms for his own use.

By way of footnote, and in fairness to American music, it should be said that long before any of this European interest was manifested at least one American 'serious' composer had attempted, with some success, to incorporate elements of American popular music into his work. This was the virtuoso pianist Louis Moreau Gottschalk (1829–69), born in New Orleans of an English–Jewish father and a French–Creole mother. His work as a composer was extremely uneven, some of it salon music of great wateriness, but he wrote a number of strongly rhythmic piano pieces which make intelligent and pleasing use of popular dance rhythms. These include the *Bamboula*, *Pasquinade*, the *Souvenir de Puerto Rico* (*Marche des Gibaros*) and, possibly the best of all, a piece called *The Banjo* whose final section recalls Stephen Foster's famous song *De Camptown Races*. But Gottschalk's isolated experiments were not followed up, and American composers in general continued to produce weak imitations of European models until the appearance of Ives, Gershwin, Copland and Thomson.

Such, then, were some of the strands which, often interwoven, influenced the young composers of the 1920s.

2

Music and the Ballet

De la musique avant toute chose.
—Verlaine

D'abord, il y eut la danse.
—Colette

Many of the works to be considered in this book were written for the stage, as operas or ballets. Apart from certain regrettable occasions when the producer is given entirely his own way (the Visconti *Traviata* at Covent Garden is a case in point) it is usually agreed that the prime considerations in opera should be musical ones. Where ballet is concerned, there is, rightly or wrongly, no such agreement. Many of the finest compositions of the 1920s took the form of ballet scores, and some general reflections on the subject of music and the ballet are therefore in order.

The vast majority of the important ballets of the 1920s received their first performances in France, at Paris or at Monte Carlo. In Germany, at least until the arrival there of the late John Cranko and Kenneth Macmillan, ballet occupied a very inferior place in the theatre. Typically, the ballet-mistress of a local opera house would be allowed a couple of evenings, perhaps, towards the end of the season, in which to show her paces, her normal role being the provision of *ballabili* for such operas as *Aïda* or *I Vespri Siciliani*. Anxious to make the most of her brief moment, the good lady would tend to offer a somewhat over-ambitious *Ballett-Abend* consisting, say, of Debussy's *Jeux*, the *Sacre* and *Daphnis and Chloe* in her own choreographic versions, based, as like as not, on the principles of Rudolf Laban, Kurt Jooss or Mary Wigman. This sort of thing, understandably, gave ballet a bad name in Germany, and though the German composers of the 1920s occasionally wrote music for dance spectacles they rarely gave them the same attention that they devoted to their operas. This was not new: Strauss's *Josefslegende* is vastly inferior to *Elektra*; *Schlag-obers* cannot bear comparison with *Intermezzo*.

In France things were very different. Until Diaghilev died in 1929, his *Ballets Russes* continually needed new scores. A rich Swede, Rolf de Maré (1888–1964), founded in 1920 a rival company, the Swedish Ballet. Between 1920 and 1925 it gave nearly 2,800 performances of twenty-four ballets, not only in Paris, but in London, New York, Barcelona, Brussels, Vienna, Budapest, Stockholm, Italy, Germany and the French provinces. De Maré's principal dancer, Jean Borlin (1893–1930), was also his choreographer. Lacking dancers as brilliant as those Diaghilev could boast, and without the choreographic talent Diaghilev could call on, in the persons of Massine, Nijinska and Balanchine, de Maré relied even more heavily than the Russian impresario on the use of *avant-garde* designers and musicians (to the point where the dancing was sometimes quite swamped, as also happened, though more rarely, with the *Ballets Russes*). Thus he was an active patron of composers.

There were other, more ephemeral companies, such as that formed by Count Etienne de Beaumont, initially to give private performances for the pleasure of the Count and his friends, later to give public ones at the Théâtre de la Cigale in 1924 and 1925. In 1933 the Englishman Edward James, continuing the tradition, founded a short-lived company called the *Ballets 1933*, which commissioned new works and gave performances in Paris and London. There was thus much activity in the ballet world, and a continual outlet for composers.

The composer is faced with a dilemma in writing music for ballet: shall he put his best into the work, or shall he, bearing in mind that ballet is one of the most ephemeral of the arts, write something that will do for the purpose, but no more?

At the cost of being, perhaps, a shade obvious, it is worth considering what it is that endows a ballet with life. What keeps a ballet in the repertory over a period of many years, or, failing that, what ensures that it preserves its freshness when it is revived? The answer would seem to be good music and good choreography, *in that order*: not a statement likely to appeal to the average balletomane. There are exceptions: it

is not their music which has preserved *Giselle* and *La Sylphide*.
Yet how much superb Petipa choreography must have been
lost, simply because the scores that accompanied it were not
the work of a genius like Tchaikovsky but that of a hack like
Minkus? The weakness of the music is surely the reason why
so few ballets have survived from the nineteenth century. And
most of it is weak, despite the efforts of such as Mr Richard
Bonynge, who has recently turned his attention in part from
breathing life, personally and vicariously, into the operas of
the early *ottocento* to attempting to perform a similar operation
on the ballet music of some minor nineteenth-century
composers. But his kiss of life has not proved efficacious: the
patient was never alive in the first place. One could point,
I suppose, to *Don Quixote* as another exception: yet if that
ballet, still performed, ever was a work of art (which I beg
leave to doubt), it is certainly not so now; which is not to say
that the way in which Vasiliev dances in it is not, on its own
and aside from the ballet, art.

Yet good music alone cannot save a ballet if satisfactory
choreography has not been devised for it. *Daphnis and Chloe*,
a superb score, by all accounts defeated Fokine, and, to be
honest, Ashton did not entirely succeed with it: a fact recognised
at its premiere in 1951 but somewhat obscured later in the
cloud of general adulation which has descended on Sir Frederick. He also had the advantage of a superb Chloe in Margot
Fonteyn, whose ability to project in this role has never been
approached by any other dancer. For her Ashton created
very fine choreography, and his opening *Danse religieuse* is one
of his most beautiful concepts (as it is one of Ravel's). But the
cumulative excitement of the final *Danse générale* found little
echo on the stage, and the *Danse guerrière* saw Ashton providing choreography which suggested *The Pirates of Penzance* and
the *Polovtsian Dances* from *Prince Igor* at one and the same time.
The effect was unconvincing and comic, and all Fonteyn's
acting ability never quite made one believe that her virginity
was in any sort of danger from this particular pirate band.

Is it, then, that Ravel's score is simply too good for the ballet
theatre? In a different case, Satie's music for *Parade* seems to
have drawn nothing but triviality from Massine. On a far
lower level than either, Milhaud's charming music for *Salade*

produced no corresponding sparkle on the stage when Peter Darrell attempted a revival at the Edinburgh Festival of 1961.

Perhaps, in the case of Ravel's masterpiece, the reason lies in the fact that the two great group dances mentioned, the *Danse guerrière* and the *Danse générale*, are characterised by cumulative excitement, continually building, and choreographers find great difficulty in matching this with something meaningful, and, as it were, *necessary*. At all events many of us would far prefer to listen to the music in the concert hall, or on gramophone records. Yet there are rare cases when ballet music, properly performed, makes more effect in the theatre than elsewhere. I am thinking in particular of *Les Noces*, which, especially in a forward recording, can weary the ear with its insistent percussiveness, but which when listened to in conjunction with the choreographic spectacle makes an overwhelming effect.

The question of performance is a vital one. When a composer has entrusted an important work to the ballet stage, the least that can be done is to perform it worthily. This is too often far from being the practice. For the lover of music a visit to the ballet is an experience fraught with aesthetic hazard. Sometimes this is due to unmusicality on the part of the choreographer. Balanchine, sometimes (*Symphonie Concertante, Theme and Variations*), despite his reputation as one of the most musical of choreographers; Macmillan, frequently (*Danses concertantes, Olympiad*); and Serge Lifar (*passim*) spring to mind as offenders in this respect. But far more often the disagreeable experiences can be laid squarely at the door of the ballet conductor, a class of person more often than not neither fish, flesh nor good red herring. This is not a new development: in the 1950s the late John Hollingsworth, by all accounts an amiable and intelligent man, regularly demonstrated in the Covent Garden pit the truth of Beecham's axiom that some conductors were born and others were Hollingsworth. So music-lovers who wince today as Mr X tears Tchaikovsky to tatters or staggers uncertainly through Stravinsky have at least the consolation that others, too, have suffered in their day.

Part of the trouble arises from the fact that it is hard to conceive of a musically talented child saying to himself, at the time when the rest of us are nourishing an ambition to be

engine drivers: 'When I grow up, I want to be a ballet
conductor.' A conductor, yes; an opera conductor, quite
possibly; a ballet conductor, no. If one studies the passing-out
lists from the military college at Sandhurst one usually finds,
at the very end, after the names of men destined for regiments
in the army, those of a few souls posted to the Royal Air Force
Regiment. I have heard it said, I do not know with what truth,
that these are the men that the army does not want and whom
it is therefore palming off on the unfortunate Royal Air
Force. It seems to me that some become ballet conductors by
an analogous process.

   This is not always true. Diaghilev employed some conductors
of very high calibre indeed: Ansermet, Beecham, Roger
Desormière, Eugene Goossens, André Messager. The conductor of the Swedish Ballet was Désiré-Emile Inghelbrecht,
who had been in charge of the premiere of Debussy's *Le
Martyre de Saint-Sébastien* and who was himself a composer of
some note (though during his brief engagement by Diaghilev,
later on, his *tempi* gave great trouble to the dancers). De Basil
employed Antal Dorati; Yuri Fayer and Rozhdestvensky
conducted ballet for the Bolshoi. Constant Lambert was a
fine conductor.

   Diaghilev looks like an exemplar in this respect: it was not
even a case of employing, near the beginning of their careers,
men who might have been expected after acquiring some fame
to move on to other fields, more rewarding in terms of acclaim
for a musician. Ansermet, Beecham and Messager were very
well-established conductors in the 1920s. Yet outside Paris,
and to some degree London, Diaghilev's musical standards
slipped. It was partly a money matter: in his later, leaner
years Diaghilev tried to recover elsewhere the money which
he spent on his Paris seasons, very expensive but very prestigious and therefore necessary to him. This meant economies,
some of them musical. It will be recalled that Ravel engaged
in indignant correspondence when Diaghilev omitted the
choral parts from the score of *Daphnis and Chloe* during the
work's London performances. When Stravinsky, somewhat
over-dramatically, referred to ballet as 'the anathema of
Christ', he is likely to have been thinking of standards of
musical performance rather than 'taking up moral attitudes',

as Noël Coward put it. Even at Monte Carlo Diaghilev was not above using conductors of distinctly low calibre, like, for instance, the now forgotten Marc-César Scotto, who, said Lambert, conducted 'like a porpoise in a rough sea'. In Paris Messager or Desormière would be engaged to conduct the same scores.

The problem, then, is a perennial one. An honourable exception among living musicians is Robert Irving, who seemed no more than competent during his days with the Sadler's Wells Ballet, but who blossomed when taken on by Balanchine as musical director of the New York City Ballet. He won golden opinions in London during the New York City Ballet's visit in the 1960s by taking the Covent Garden Orchestra with complete security through complex and unfamiliar music such as the Webern scores used by Balanchine.

The conductor cannot, however, bear the whole responsibility. Orchestral musicians are, after all, supposed to possess an artistic conscience (a belief sometimes hard to sustain after a few hours' conversation with some of them). The conductor must work through an orchestra. One can find excuses for the players. Take, for instance, the hard-working Orchestra of the Royal Opera House, Covent Garden, playing, probably, seven performances a week forty-eight weeks a year. One cannot perhaps entirely blame them, if having, let us say, played *Elektra* on a Tuesday, they feel disposed to take it easy when confronted the following night with *Le Lac des cygnes* in its 500th or 600th performance since 1946—the more particularly as the players are well aware that much of the ballet audience is musically illiterate and has come, in any case, not to listen to Tchaikovsky but to see Rudolf Nureyev. The phenomenon does not seem universal: the Orchestra of the Royal Theatre in Copenhagen seems well aware that it has a treasure in its hands when it plays, for instance, *Cassenoisette*. On the other hand it plays far less than the Covent Garden Orchestra.

I have gone into this matter at some length because it is crucial to the status of ballet as an art: if it is an art, even a major art, as some claim, all its component parts are important, and not least the music. I might add that there is a limit to the usefulness and interest of ballets danced in practice dress,

ballets danced to Chopin piano pieces, strung together, and
other devices for enabling economy to masquerade as simplicity or 'classicism'. Furthermore it is high time for those in
positions of authority to show some confidence in the art they
practise and begin once again, as a regular custom, to commission ballet scores from living composers rather than resort-
ing to the music of men safely dead and unable to speak for
themselves: the Massenet mishmash assembled for Macmillan's
Manon was a particularly unworthy way of accompanying
what was presumably intended as a major exercise in self-
rehabilitation if not in choreography.

For better or worse many, indeed almost all, of the composers dealt with in these pages worked in the field of ballet.
Many of them accomplished beautiful and important work
there. This will never be recognised properly until such of their
works as are revived are accorded performances worthy of
them in the theatre as well as in the concert hall and on
gramophone records.

3

Neoclassicism

Classicism is health, romanticism is sickness.

—Goethe

L'élégance consiste à ne pas étonner.

—Cocteau

During the winter of 1918–19 Diaghilev gave Stravinsky a large bundle of music and asked him to arrange and orchestrate enough of it to fit a libretto drawn from a *commedia dell'arte* play of which Massine had recently found the text. The music was all by or attributed to the eighteenth-century Neapolitan composer Pergolesi, and Diaghilev had assembled it himself during research in Italian libraries. At least one other composer, Vincenzo Tommasini, had already carried out such an exercise for Diaghilev. The result, derived from the music of Domenico Scarlatti, had been the ballet *The Good-Humoured Ladies*, with choreography by Massine and sets by Bakst, first seen at the Teatro Costanzi in Rome on 12 April, 1917. While Stravinsky was working on the Pergolesi pieces, Ottorino Respighi was busy converting *Le astuzie femminili*, by Cimarosa, from an opera to an opera-ballet. This was eventually presented at the Paris Opéra on 27 May, 1920, again with Massine choreography and with sets and costumes by José-Maria Sert. It did not last long in the repertory, and was soon converted into a ballet pure and simple under the title *Cimarosiana*. Neither of these works made a great deal of musical impact, though *The Good-Humoured Ladies* was a notable balletic success, for both Tommasini's and Respighi's treatments were of a tactful, unstartling nature. Stravinsky's work was very different: the result was *Pulcinella*.

It would seem that Diaghilev had little idea of what Stravinsky was up to. He told his choreographer, Massine, that the music would be scored for what he described, rather quaintly, as 'a large orchestra with harps'. In fact what emerged was a ballet with songs in one act and eight scenes scored for three vocal soloists—soprano, tenor and bass—and an orchestra of chamber proportions. The principal sources were twelve Trio Sonatas and two operas, *Il fratello innamorato* and *Il Flaminio*.

The ballet was first performed during the same season as *Le astuzie femminili*, twelve days before it, on 15 May, 1920, and it was a huge success. Massine had apparently created excellent choreography, and Picasso's designs were much admired. The impact of the music resounded throughout the entire decade that followed, for Stravinsky had not been content with tactful rearrangement: he had virtually recomposed the music, and the score that resulted was as much Stravinsky as Pergolesi: in fact rather more. Stravinsky's treatment aroused indignation among musicians: he was said to have done violence to Pergolesi, and thirteen years later Lambert attacked the deliberate incongruities of the score, comparing them to the curious juxtapositions of subject-matter in the paintings of the surrealist Max Ernst. Yet today the exercise seems perfectly legitimate: the eighteenth-century crispness of Pergolesi and the twentieth-century crispness of Stravinsky sit well together, and the result is light, elegant and gay. For true incongruity one must turn to Richard Strauss's elephantine treatment of Lully in the incidental music to *Le Bourgeois Gentilhomme* or his similar exercises at the expense of the unfortunate Couperin.

In speaking of the 'influence' of *Pulcinella* it is important to make it absolutely clear what one means. It is wrong to think of musicians rushing to follow Stravinsky's example by 're-composing' eighteenth-century scores. This occurred very little. For instance, when H. Casadesus went to work on the music of Montéclair (1666–1737) the result was quite anodyne. This was *Les Tentations de la bergère ou l'amour vainqueur* (choreo-graphy—Nijinska, sets and costumes—Juan Gris, first per-formance—Monte Carlo, 3 January, 1924). Similarly, when Jean Françaix re-orchestrated *Scuola di ballo* for Colonel de Basil's Company (the ballet had originally been performed during the *Soirées de Paris* in May 1924), his treatment of Boccherini for this charming adaptation of a Goldoni comedy was very tactful. Lambert's arrangements of Boyce produced a result that was Boyce, not Lambert. Only two 're-compositions' on *Pulcinella* lines spring to mind, and both came much later.

Both were by members of *Les Six*. In 1937 Milhaud made his own version of *The Beggar's Opera*, *L'Opéra des gueux*, in a translation by Louis Ducreux, for a broadcast by Radio Marseille. From it, as was often his habit where his incidental music was concerned, he extracted an orchestral suite which he called *Le Carnaval de Londres*. This subjects the original melodies to fairly cavalier treatment, notably in the *Bal-ouverture*, which is a rollicking samba consisting of repetitions in various keys of the tune *Over the hills and far away*. There is also a charming version of *Lilliburlero* called *Sur la Tamise*. It is a most engaging work. Two years earlier, Poulenc had been asked to write incidental music for a production of a play by Edouard Bourdet, *La Reine Margot*. He decided to base his music on the compositions of the sixteenth-century composer Claude Gervaise, and, like Milhaud, he extracted a suite from it, the *Suite française*. This is scored for a small group of instruments, including harpsichord (there is also a version for solo piano), and includes a *Bransle de Bourgogne*, a *Pavane*, a *Petite marche militaire*, a *Complainte*, a *Bransle de Champagne*, a *Sicilienne* and a movement Poulenc called *Carillon*. The music critic David Drew has referred to this Suite as illiterate trifling; I confess to finding it most enjoyable. But neither the Milhaud nor the Poulenc work is of the importance and impact of *Pulcinella*: both are minor.

There also continued to be essays in pastiche writing for specific dramatic purposes, on the lines of Tchaikovsky's Mozartian pastiche in *The Queen of Spades* or the cantata in Act 2 of *Tosca*. For example, in his ballet *Cydalise et le chèvre-pied* (Paris Opéra, 15 January, 1923) Gabriel Pierné, writing in general for a very large orchestra (quadruple woodwind with extra flutes, much percussion, two harps, mixed chorus and so on) reduced it sharply to a small group with harpsichord for the courtly *Ballet de la Sultane des Indes*. Similarly, though less mellifluously, Honegger introduced into his *Jeanne d'Arc au bûcher* (completed in 1935, and first performed in concert version under Paul Sacher at Basle on 12 May, 1938) a neoclassic ballet episode called *Les Rois ou l'invention du jeu de cartes*.

But despite the paucity of direct influence there is no doubt that *Pulcinella* spearheaded the neoclassic movement. It

affected musicians in various ways. In general it can be said
to have contributed towards a movement in favour of spareness
of outline, modesty of aim and emphasis on tunes. Among a
number of French composers it led to what might be described
as a return to the elegant hedonism of the eighteenth century.
There is much of this spirit in Poulenc's *Les Biches*, which will
be discussed elsewhere, and whose finale is a very close echo
of the closing pages of *Pulcinella*. But in *Les Biches* and scores of
its type the eighteenth-century influence was mixed with
others. Introducing a recording, made in 1972, of five of
Diaghilev's 'French' ballets, Igor Markevitch said: 'They are
united by a certain tone, into which there enter the French
chanson, the eighteenth century, the *café-concert*, Bizet's zest, a
touch of Chabrier, some of Schumann's tenderness, and the
sordid splendour of the circus'. It certainly sounds a proper
muddle, and Lambert's *Music Ho!* contains a devastating
though brief analysis of *Les Biches* on these lines, in which
Lambert suggests that Poulenc jumps from style to style with
bewildering speed in order to avoid seeming 'dated' at any
point. Much as I admire Lambert's keen intelligence, I cannot
follow him here. What he says has a certain truth, but he
chooses to ignore the fact that the result is marked from start
to finish with Poulenc's personal style, and, although opinions
are subjective, the work seems to me a minor masterpiece (and
in balletic terms a major one).

A typical example of a French 'neoclassic' ballet is Auric's
Les Fâcheux (Monte Carlo, 19 January, 1924, with choreography by Nijinska and sets and costumes by Braque; Massine
made new choreography for Diaghilev in 1927). Auric,
Cocteau said, using an expression of the Midi, *parlait pointu*:
his pen scratched and tore at the paper. Certainly throughout
Auric's career his music has possessed a certain sharpness and
acidity, found in early scores such as this and also in his later
film scores for Cocteau, such as that for the superb *Orphée*.
The idea for *Les Fâcheux* sprang from a visit Diaghilev paid to
the Théâtre de l'Odéon in 1922. They were performing
Molière's *comédie-ballet* of the same name, which the dramatist
had conceived, written and staged in a fortnight. The idea of
the play is extremely simple: a man, on his way to an amorous
assignation, is repeatedly prevented from getting there by a

series of '*fâcheux*' or bores. Each of its three acts ends with a ballet. At the suggestion of the actor Pierre Bertin, a close friend and colleague of the musical *Nouveaux Jeunes*, Paul Gavault, the Director of the Odéon, had commissioned music for the three ballets from Auric. After seeing the play, Diaghilev asked Auric to expand his music to make it into a ballet for the Russian company to dance. Auric's score, in no way of the calibre of *Les Biches* or Milhaud's *La Création du monde*, is an agreeable, professional piece of work which, without using seventeenth- or eighteenth-century material, exhales a very similar atmosphere which is appropriate to the subject. The influence of Stravinsky is marked. A blander instance of neoclassicism is the little *Piano Concertino* written in 1932 by Jean Françaix, then twenty years old, and first played by him at a Lamoureux Concert (15 December, 1934). It is a classic instance of the manufacture of pleasant and decorative bricks with the absolute minimum of straw.

Several works which Poulenc wrote in the 1920s are more strongly neoclassic in feeling than *Les Biches*. One of them is the *Trio* for piano, oboe and bassoon, written in 1926 and dedicated to Manuel de Falla. This shows the direct influence of Stravinsky and the indirect influence of Haydn, Poulenc's model for the introductory *Presto*. But, as in Ravel's *Piano Concerto in G*, there is another influence in the *Trio*: that of Saint-Saëns, in the *Trio's* final *Rondo*, whose bouncy triple time is modelled on the scherzo of Saint-Saëns' *Second Piano Concerto*.

Both Poulenc and de Falla wrote Harpsichord Concerti for Wanda Landowska, the gifted and masterful woman whose efforts were responsible for the rehabilitation of the harpsichord as a concert instrument.

By the time he came to write his *Concerto* Manuel de Falla's music had changed a great deal from his early manner. His first ballet, *El amor brujo*, had been written in the Andalusian style, appropriately enough, since its first exponent on stage had been the great Pastora Imperio (Teatro Lara, Madrid, 15 April, 1915). The following year Diaghilev signed a contract with Falla. The Spaniard engaged to deliver what was eventually to be *The Three-Cornered Hat*, a ballet by Martinez Sierra based on the story by Alarcón. Diaghilev was in no

position to present the ballet in 1917 (it was in the spring of
that year that Falla finished his first version of the score). It
was therefore performed in Spain, with Diaghilev's permission,
as a mime accompanied by chamber orchestra under the title
El corregidor y la molinera (Teatro Eslava, Madrid, 7 April,
1917). The final version received its first performance under
Ansermet at the Alhambra Theatre in London on 22 July, 1919.
It was in London that Falla, at Diaghilev's request, added the
Miller's Dance or *Farruca*, as well as the electrifying opening.
Those who have seen the ballet will remember that before the
curtain rises there is a fanfare on trumpets and drums,
followed by clapping, castanets, *Olés*, and the voice of a
flamenco singer. Falla's score for *The Three-Cornered Hat* has a
sharpness and incisiveness which were new in his work. The
imaginative use of an orchestral piano gives an added crispness
to the sound. Already his music was moving towards his final
manner, crystallised in two works, *El retablo de Maese Pedro*
and the *Harpsichord Concerto* already mentioned, where
Castilian dryness (which is not to imply aridity) mingles with
a certain Stravinskian quality.

The *Rétable* (as the work was known in France) was written
between 1919 and 1922 and first given, in concert form, under
the composer's bâton at Seville on 23 March, 1923. For its
first performance as a puppet-opera (it is based on an episode
in *Don Quixote*) it had to wait only three months more. On 23
June it was given under Vladimir Golschmann, with Wanda
Landowska playing the important harpsichord part, in the
salon of the Princesse Edmond de Polignac, in Paris.

The mention of the Princesse de Polignac prompts some
reflection on the large role private money and patronage
played in the musical and artistic life of the period in France.
This feature did not disappear with the 1920s, though it
diminished, as private fortunes themselves contracted. In his
introduction to *The Paris Diary of Ned Rorem** Robert Phelps,
speaking of the early 1950s, when Rorem went to live in the
French capital, writes that 'it was not unknown for a great
lady to offer a young composer the use of her salon for a
concert and to invite a hundred people who had once heard
Stravinsky and Ravel play their own music in the same

* *The Paris Diary of Ned Rorem*, New York and London, 1966/7.

precincts'. This was very true, but things went much further. Rolf de Maré and Edward James founded their own ballet companies, as we have seen. Chanel poured money into Diaghilev's enterprises. But three great names in particular stand out for a support only matched, among private people at that time, by Mrs Elizabeth Sprague Coolidge in the U.S., whose commissions included Stravinsky's *Apollon musagète*, Respighi's *Trittico Botticelliano*, and the *Chansons madécasses* of Ravel. Those names are Polignac, Beaumont and Noailles.

Marie-Laure de Noailles and her husband Charles were directly responsible, among other works, for the *Aubade* of Poulenc and his cantata *Le Balmasqué*, for the Dali-Buñuel film *L'Age d'or* and the Cocteau film (his first) *Le Sang d'un poète*. Etienne de Beaumont underwrote the Milhaud-Cocteau spectacle *Le Boeuf sur le Toit* and ultimately, as has been mentioned, supported his own ballet company during the *Soirées de Paris*. The Princesse Edmond de Polignac (born Winnaretta Singer, of the American sewing-machine manufacturing company) had a hand in the creation of Satie's *Socrate*, Stravinsky's *Le Renard*, Poulenc's *Concertos* for two pianos and for organ, Falla's *Retablo*, Milhaud's *Les Malheurs d'Orphée*, Weill's *Symphony No. 2* and works by Fauré. Diaghilev presented Stravinsky's *Oedipus Rex* under her patronage. I have mentioned only some examples. It would be a dull, puritanical soul, terrified of glitter and glamour, who failed to salute so laudable and splendid a use of money. All praise to those who gave it.

The tone set by Falla's little puppet-opera was continued and intensified in the *Harpsichord Concerto in D major*, which he completed in 1926 and dedicated to Landowska, who played it for the first time in Barcelona on 4 November that year with an ensemble under Pablo Casals. During the time that he had been composing it Falla had spent an Easter in Seville with Garcia Lorca, and while there he had heard in an early morning procession an ensemble of oboes and bassoons which made an intense impression on him. He also heard in Seville the great bell-sounds which were to toll in the second movement of the *Concerto*. He scored the work for harpsichord and a small ensemble of flute, oboe, clarinet, violin and 'cello; during its composition the French and neoclassic influences on Falla were absorbed completely, and the final result was utterly Spanish. Despite its extreme brevity the *Concerto* has a claim to be considered one of the few great musical achievements ever to have emerged from Spain.

Poulenc's concerto, a very different affair, had sprung from the Paris performance of the *Rétable*. Poulenc helped during rehearsals: his friend and teacher the pianist Ricardo Viñes was operating the puppets. Landowska ordered (rather than asked) Poulenc to write her a concerto. The young Frenchman set to work. A largely self-taught musician, he had much to learn about the technique of the harpsichord. Yet he contrived to make a success of the work, which he wrote during 1927–8. He called it the *Concert champêtre*. During his childhood he had spent summer holidays at his grandmother's house at Nogent-sur-Marne, at the eastern end of the Bois de Vincennes, and he explained that for him the word *champêtre* conveyed suburbia (not, one feels, in the English sense: one cannot associate harpsichord concerti with Hatch End or Rickmansworth). Landowska, as it happens, was living at the time the work was composed at Saint-Leu-la-Forêt, not far from Ermenonville, where every Sunday in spring she gave recitals in a studio built among the trees in her garden. It was in such an atmosphere that Poulenc placed his work: it was to be rural in the sense that Diderot would have used the term. Some days before the first public performance, Landowska and Poulenc gave a private one at Saint-Leu, the composer taking the orchestral part on a piano. The first public performance was at the Salle Pleyel in Paris on 3 May, 1929, with the Orchestre Symphonique de Paris under Pierre Monteux.

A severe, highly Stravinskian introduction precedes the *Allegro molto* which forms the main body of the first movement. During the course of preparing a television documentary about Poulenc, the music populariser John Amis visited le Grand Coteau, the composer's country house at Noizay in the Touraine. He noticed that on Poulenc's piano there stood a photograph of Stravinsky at his most severe and forbidding. Amis imagined Poulenc at work, composing 'at the piano' in the manner much disapproved of by some, trying out, perhaps, something in his most 'galant', French style; then suddenly looking up and becoming aware of the Russian master's baleful stare. Could this, Amis wondered, be the explanation for the sudden appearances in Poulenc's work of those acidly harmonised wind passages that one encounters from time to time? Were they a sop to the Russian Cerberus? At all events, such episodes are a striking feature of Poulenc's work. There is a conspicuous example in the interlude between the two acts of the *opéra-bouffe Les Mamelles de Tirésias* (1944): the lugubrious, chorale-like passage immediately preceding an extremely 'common' march marked by raucous chromatic descents on the brass.

The mood of severity is sustained a little longer at the opening of the *Concert champêtre*, but before too long the brisk, cheerful *Allegro* begins. The *Andante*, a *siciliana*, with its Mozartian blend of calm and emotion, is perhaps the finest thing in the concerto, while the finale (*Presto: très gai*) is a helter-skelter affair which pauses just before its end to return to the solemn mood of the beginning.

The critic Gabriel Marcel claimed to have detected 'barrack calls' in the finale and also, to some degree, in the *Allegro molto*. Poulenc explained that in his youth the bugles of the Fort de Vincennes, heard from the wood nearby, were to him as poetic as hunting horns in a vast forest had been to Weber. Well and good, if that is how it strikes you. The description suggests those distant bugles that play so large a part in the brilliant but haunted writings of Jocelyn Brooke, bugles whose calls evoke a strange, remote, fascinating, frightening, masculine world. Poulenc's bugle calls evoke a masculine world too: but they convey the cheerful proximity (and possibly even availability) of agreeably rude and licentious soldiery.

At all events they are not the result of a psychological trigger-reaction, like the outbursts of popular and military music in Mahler. A heavy responsibility must rest on the shoulders of those street musicians who happened to be playing when Mahler *père* was beating Mahler *mère* up. The echo of their music resounds in a thousand concert halls. If only they had known what havoc they were wreaking one feels that they might have broken off till they were safely out of earshot of the Mahler establishment. (Likewise, one cannot help wondering if the Turks at Deraa had any notion of the literary *fracas* they were stirring up when they did whatever it was they did do to T. E. Lawrence.) Poulenc, though not without his sadnesses and his heartbreaks, had a cheerfulness and humour totally absent, so far as one can tell, in both Mahler and Lawrence. This does not mean that he was not from the start a serious person: the concept that he began as a *gamin* and turned into a religious mystic is a false one. He was both from the beginning.

Poulenc's way of dealing with a private grief is well illustrated in a work, one of his finest, which was written in 1929 and first performed at one of those lavish entertainments that were so typical a feature of Paris in the 1920s. Like the *Concert champêtre*, it is to some degree 'neoclassic'. This is the *Aubade*: a choreographic concerto for piano and eighteen instruments.

Ned Rorem once wrote, with pardonable exaggeration, that *le tout Paris* consisted of seventy-five people (he hastened to add that he had met them all). At all events the fancy-dress ball which Charles and Marie-Laure de Noailles gave in the garden of their Paris house (covered in for the purpose) on 18 June, 1929, had just eighty guests. As one of the entertainments for these fortunate people the Noailles had commissioned Poulenc to write a ballet, which was presented with choreography by Nijinska and décor and costumes by Jean-Michel Frank. Poulenc played the solo piano part, and Vladimir Golschmann conducted the small orchestra. This consisted of two flutes, two oboes, two clarinets, two bassoons, two horns, trumpet, timpani, two violas (no violins), two 'cellos and two double-basses. The predominance of woodwind colouring underlined the melancholy sensuality of the score.

The concerto which Poulenc had written for his patrons (and which he dedicated to the Vicomtesse) was easy on the ear: it was totally suitable for the occasion and it gave immediate pleasure to its hearers. Yet, despite the animation of a number of its movements, it was far from superficial and, in essence, melancholy.

Poulenc later wrote of it as follows:

At a period of my life when I was feeling very sad I found that dawn was the time when my anguish reached its height, for it meant that one had to live through another horrible day. I wanted to give a detached rendering of this impression, so I chose Diana as my symbolic heroine. She, a goddess and a beautiful woman, was doomed to perpetual chastity among women, with no other distraction than the chase. Every day the goddess must reluctantly resume her hunting in the forest, carrying the bow that was as tedious to her as my piano was at that time to me.*

The crucial words are: *I wanted to give a detached rendering of this impression.* Poulenc was in many ways a truly classical artist, able to stand back from his own personal situations and predicaments and to use them in a detached way as a medium for his art. Thus, for instance, when his close friend the composer Pierre-Octave Ferroud was killed in particularly horrible circumstances (he was decapitated in a car accident), Poulenc was moved to compose his beautiful *Litanies à la Vierge noire de Rocamadour*, a work which in its brief span (it lasts no more than eight minutes) crystallises the essentials of Poulenc's religious style. In the case of the *Aubade*, Diana, doomed to the society of women, was a meaningful choice. Poulenc, as is well known, was homosexually inclined, and, though homosexuality as often as not appears to doom men to perpetual unchastity rather than the reverse, he was thus debarred from the physical love of women and the pleasures of parenthood.

I can, I fear, cast no light on the reasons for the composer's depression at this time in his life; nor can his biographer, Henri Hell. But one's guess is that the causes were emotional in character; they cannot have been financial, for Poulenc was never poor, nor can they have been connected with lack of professional success, since Poulenc's was not a musical career marked by struggles for popularity and acceptance. Certainly the aforementioned sensuality of the score suggests an atmosphere of erotic restlessness.

The action, then, is simple: Diana awakes at dawn; her companions try to distract her, but in vain; and she departs, bored and depressed, for the chase. The movements are as follows:

Toccata: Lento e pesante
Récitatif: Larghetto: *Les compagnes de Diane*

* Francis Poulenc on his ballets, *Ballet*, September 1946.

Rondeau: Allegro: *Diane et ses compagnes*
Presto: *Toilette de Diane*
Récitatif: Larghetto: *Introduction à la variation de Diane*
Andante: *Variation de Diane*
Allegro feroce: *Désespoir de Diane*
Conclusion: Adagio: *Adieux et départ de Diane*

After an introductory orchestral flourish the solo piano embarks on a brilliant toccata. The following *Récitatif*, like the other woodwind-dominated interjections in the work, has an operatic feeling. The music pursues its way in distinct numbers of varying sweetness and acerbity, the latter reaching its height in the penultimate *Allegro feroce*, a brief but violent movement which conveys a feeling of acute mental frustration and physical irritation. Its mood recalls the words of another mythological heroine who suffered from erotic frustration, Phaedra, on her first appearance in Racine's play of that name:

> *Que ces vains ornements, que ces voiles me pèsent!*
> *Quelle importune main, en formant tous ces noeuds,*
> *A pris soin sur mon front d'assembler mes cheveux?*
> *Tout m'afflige et me nuit, et conspire à me nuire.*

Everything, too, seems to conspire to irritate and wound Diana. The final movement, introduced by more woodwind calls, returns to the opening flourish. Its music maintains a processional, steady tread, reinforced by timpani strokes, superbly conveying a feeling of weary resignation.

It is sad to have to tell the subsequent history of the work. Poulenc was delighted with Nijinska's treatment of his ballet, but on no other occasion did a production satisfy him. Other choreographers saw inadequate 'action' in the subject of the ballet as planned by the composer, and felt impelled to 'jazz it up'. First in the field was Balanchine, who opted, like other choreographers since, to introduce a male character in the form of Actaeon and to make of the ballet a telling of the story of his love for Diana and its unhappy end. The music is quite unsuited to this. In his own words, Poulenc was 'weak enough' to permit this treatment, and this was the version seen at the Théâtre des Champs-Elysées at the work's first public staged performance by the Nemchinova-Dolin Company (21 January, 1930). Poulenc mentioned this version in the printed score, but also gave his own version, hoping, he said, that future choreographers would have the wit to choose his. But in his *Diana* at Copenhagen in 1933 Harald Lander followed where Balanchine had led.

Worst of all, the ballet eventually fell into the hands of Serge Lifar, who brought the dinner-jacketed musicians on to the stage with inappropriate and lamentable effect. This was the version seen in London during the season of Lifar's short-lived *Nouveau Ballet de Monte Carlo* at the Cambridge Theatre in July 1946 (when Renée Jeanmaire and Vladimir Skouratoff took the principal parts) and later in the season of the company of the Marquis de Cuevas at Covent Garden in 1948 (with Marjorie Tallchief and George Skibine).

I have written earlier about the unmusicality of certain choreographers, notably Lifar. His 1946 London season provided further demonstration, if such were needed, of this, among them an extraordinary 'utility' *Afternoon of a Faun*, with Lifar but without nymphs, a comic performance the like of which I have never seen matched on the ballet stage (though a close rival was Anton Dolin's *entrée*, all feathers and spangles, as *Le Roi Soleil:* a piece danced to what seemed to be every single Ancient Air and Dance from all three of Respighi's Sets, and which reduced at least one house to helpless merriment). Lifar's *Faun* was sad as well as funny: this, then, one thought, as one looked at a rather podgy, middle-aged man, was *le dieu de la danse*.

Nijinska, alas, is dead; so is Poulenc. But *Aubade* is potentially so good as ballet music that it is a great pity that someone does not attempt a revival on the lines laid down by the composer, and observing his wish that the décor and costumes are to be in the style of Fontainebleau—which, he wrote bitterly, 'is no doubt why *Aubade* is generally given in a music-hall setting'. We are not so rich in good music for ballet that we can afford to ignore scores of this calibre.

Other composers too, not so directly under the influence of Stravinsky, moved towards neoclassicism. This was true of Hindemith and Weill, who will be considered on a later page. It was true of the Fauré pupil Alfredo Casella, whose most famous work was the Pirandello ballet *La Giara* (Swedish Ballet, 19 November, 1924, with sets by Chirico). This was an incursion into folklorism, but from the mid-1920s Casella became a more or less completely neoclassic composer. It was true on occasion of Prokofiev: witness his *Classical Symphony*, classic in form and feel, yet so typical of its composer that there is no feeling whatsoever of pastiche. It was however a comparatively isolated instance in Prokofiev's work, just as Bloch's first *Concerto Grosso* was a rarity in his output. This was written in 1924–5, as an exemplar, it is said, for his pupils. With its *Prelude*, *Dirge*, *Pastorale and Rustic Dances* and *Fugue*, it is a most engaging work, though even more apart from Bloch's normal darkly romantic style than is the *Classical Symphony* from Prokofiev's usual manner.

In certain of his works Arthur Honegger too moved towards neoclassicism, though Honegger was never much concerned with fashion. Despite the prevailing climate of the 1920s, he never ceased to admire such composers as Strauss, Florent Schmitt and even Max Reger. A pupil of Widor and Vincent d'Indy, Honegger's first success—and it proved a great one— was *Le Roi David*. The Swiss writer René Morax had written a festival play of this title for production at the Théâtre du Jorat at Mézières, near Lausanne. He asked Honegger (also of Swiss parentage, though born at Le Havre) to write the music. Honegger completed the score on 28 April, 1921, after nine weeks' work, and *Le Roi David* was first produced on the following 13 June. The composer rewrote it on a larger scale for concert purposes two years later. With its barbaric dances and marches, its flowing choral writing and its melodiousness, it made an immediate impression, and it is still popular with choral societies in Britain and America. *Belshazzar's Feast* owes something to it. Like much of Honegger's music throughout his career, especially the large oratorio-like works with which he is particularly associated, *Le Roi David* is extremely eclectic in style. One of its elements consists of broad choruses over a fugal orchestral texture which hark back very definitely to baroque music, in much the same way as does the chorus *O furchtbares Ereignis* (the 'typhoon' chorus) in Weill's *Mahagonny*.

An exceptionally fine example of Honegger's neoclassic

manner is to be found in the ballet *Amphion*. This is a *mélodrame* for reciter, baritone solo, four women's voices, chorus and orchestra, which the composer wrote in 1929 and which was produced at the Paris Opéra during an Ida Rubinstein season on 23 June, 1931. Ida Rubinstein, naturally, played the principal role (her influence is discussed on pp. 82–5). No expense was spared in securing a fine baritone (it was Charles Panzéra). The words were by Paul Valéry, the choreography by Massine, the sets by Alexandre Benois. Much later, Honegger extracted from the score a *Prelude, Fugue and Postlude*, which were in fact the closing pages of the ballet. During the *Prelude* Apollo gives Amphion a lyre and tells him to discover music and its power. Amphion invents the musical scales, the tempo of the music at this point changing to *Allegro marcato*. During the subsequent *Fugue* the power of music is demonstrated graphically as stones begin to move together of their own accord to form a city: Thebes. In the final section, marked *largamente*, the people wish to acclaim Amphion as divine, but a veiled woman bars their way and leads Amphion from them, after throwing his lyre into a fountain. During this episode the fugue subject is heard for the last time, very gently, on flute, harp and celesta. Obviously the ballet will never be revived as such, and probably for good reason (see pp. 82–6 on the difficulties of making *mélodrame* viable), but the music of the *Prelude, Fugue and Postlude* forms a completely satisfactory musical sequence of its own and needs no programme to give it meaning. It is not only technically expert: it is most moving.

4

Key Works of Satie and Stravinsky

Quand j'étais jeune on me disait:
Vous verrez quand vous aurez
cinquante ans. J'ai cinquante ans:
je n'ai rien vu.

—Erik Satie

Satie was born over fifty years before the beginning of the decade with which we are dealing, and it was not until three years before 1920 that he became famous. But thereafter his influence was very great.

He was born at Honfleur on 17 May, 1866, of a Scots mother and a Norman father. From the age of 21 he lived consistently in Paris, originally in Montmartre and finally in the working-class district of Arcueil. He worked as a pianist in a *cabaret artistique* called *Le Chat Noir*, run by one Rodolphe Salis, and subsequently at a similar establishment called the *Auberge du Clou*, which is where he and Debussy met. This was the period of his life from which date the *Gymnopédies* and the hardly inferior *Gnossiennes*. During the 1890s he wrote not only music for the ceremonies of the Rosicrucian cult but songs for the artists who performed at the establishments where he played the piano. These are more properly dealt with in a later chapter (see p. 47). In 1903 he composed a masterpiece, to which he gave a typically quirky title:

3 Morceaux en forme de Poire
à 4 mains
avec une Manière de Commencement,
une Prolongation du même,
et un En Plus,
suivi d'une Redite.

Too much, I think, has been made of Satie's strange titles

and his humorous instructions to the player: sometimes funny, sometimes not, they were largely defence mechanisms used by a man of great shyness. It is worth noting that in the preface to the *Heures séculaires et instantanées* Satie expressly forbade the reading aloud of these texts during performance: an instruction which, if obeyed, would torpedo many a Satie-Abend of the type rendered popular in England by the pianist Peter Dickinson.

Satie was profoundly serious and highly accomplished: as is well known, Albert Roussel, with whom Satie belatedly—and, according to Roussel, quite needlessly—studied, said of him that 'il était prodigieusement musicien'. That is why it is so misleading to compare Satie with Lord Berners. Where music was concerned, Berners was a very talented dilettante who, emotionally speaking, never emerged from the nursery, which is why the Benjamin Pollock Toy Theatre ballet he wrote for Diaghilev, *The Triumph of Neptune*, is by far his most successful work. Both this ballet and Walton's far more brilliant *Façade* seem to have been conceived in the nursery at Renishaw amid the bustle of Sir George Sitwell's three talented children, none of whom, like Peter Pan, ever grew up, artistically speaking, and all of whom continued to believe in fairies. The movement called *The Frozen Forest* in *The Triumph of Neptune*, with its so-wittily named *Schneewaldweben* section, is very revealing: it is genuine old lavender, not at all satirically meant. Berners was a gentle soul, and when Sir Frederick Ashton said that his waltzes were 'lovely' and evoked the picture of governesses sitting at upright pianos, tinkling away, he was showing the percipience to be expected of so musical a choreographer: just so they are. Berners' attempts at modernism remind one of Anthony Blanche's remark to the narrator, Charles Ryder, in *Brideshead Revisited*, when the latter is exhibiting some paintings and drawings of Latin America, thought to be very different from his usual English architectural subjects: 'It was charm again, my dear, simple, creamy English charm, playing tigers'. I have no wish to denigrate Berners' modest but agreeable talent, comparable to the water-colour work of the more talented English spinsters of the nineteenth century, and in certain pieces, such as the *Hornpipe*, *Harlequinade* and *Schottische* of *The Triumph of Neptune*, much better. But in music one must learn to separate the men from the boys, and Berners' continental exemplars were adult. Satie's music can be ferocious. Despite the charm of his music, Berners' principal gift lay in writing words rather than notes, and he must be seen in the round as writer, painter, musician and arguably the last of the great English eccentrics.

The *Trois morceaux en forme de poire* (there are seven of them, one need hardly say) for piano duet are classically balanced and have that sad tranquillity and grave simplicity (to borrow Robert Layton's words) one so often finds in the music of Satie. On hearing them, Cocteau decided that he had found the right composer for an enterprise he had in mind, the enterprise which started as *David* and ended as *Parade*.

It was after emerging from a period of belated study at the Schola Cantorum (1905–8) that Satie wrote his two chorales and two fugues, *En habit de cheval* (1911), also for piano duet. Again he was working in an area of classicism hardly explored at the time but to become crucial later on.

But Satie's greatest creations are two in number: his ballet *Parade* and his *drame symphonique* (which is neither symphonic nor dramatic, in any obvious sense), *Socrate*. It is as well to declare one's hand: there is no doubt in my mind that both, in their extremely different ways, are masterpieces.

During 1913–14 Cocteau conceived the idea of a ballet to be called *David*. It was to make use of acrobats, a clown, and various circus characters. They were to be seen in the 'parade' for *David*, a lavish spectacle that was supposed to be taking place, invisible to the audience, behind a curtain. A 'parade', it should be explained, is a series of excerpts from a show to be seen inside a booth at a fair: a 'trailer'. Cocteau put the idea to Stravinsky as possible composer, and to Diaghilev as possible impresario; neither showed much interest. In 1914 war broke out and the Diaghilev Ballet's activities were, for a time, brought to a halt. During the following year two important developments took place. Edgard Varèse introduced Cocteau to Picasso, and Cocteau heard the *Trois morceaux en forme de poire*, played by their composer and Ricardo Viñes. He decided that Satie would make an admirable composer for his project, which he had by no means abandoned. In the October of that year Valentine Gross (later Madame

Jean Hugo) brought Cocteau and Satie together. The final version of Cocteau's project saw the light of day at the Théâtre du Châtelet on 18 May, 1917, in a presentation by the Diaghilev Ballet, with sets, costumes and drop-curtain by Picasso and choreography by Massine. Ernest Ansermet conducted. In essence the final result was not so far from Cocteau's original conception: three 'Managers' (one of them a pantomime horse) and several performers (a Chinese conjuror, two acrobats and a *petite fille américaine*) try to entice the public into their booth to see the complete show; they fail to do so.

As an event, *Parade* was a major manifestation of the *avant-garde* of the period. It was also Picasso's first venture into the field of theatrical design. It created a stir. As an important artistic event it has attracted much attention from Diaghilev scholars, and there has been much learned discussion as to who contributed which idea to the final result. At times this has got a little out of hand. Take, for instance, the matter of the drop-curtain. Mrs Nesta Macdonald and others claim to have detected in this curtain a number of laborious and singularly unfunny jokes about Diaghilev and his entourage. These jokes, if such they be, are of more interest to collectors of the bin-ends of Diaghilevian tittle-tattle than to lovers of the ballet, or, for that matter, lovers of art. It is a very beautiful curtain, quite different in style from the Cubist sets it rises to reveal. These again, in their way, are beautiful, and certainly historic. It was fascinating, at the comparatively recent revivals of the ballet in New York and London, to see these sets and to see what the 'Managers', of whom one had read so much, looked like and how they moved and stamped.

Yet, as one watched, one sensed that this ballet—as a ballet—was not very good. It had not an ounce of the theatrical life exhaled by the tattiest revival of *The Three-Cornered Hat*. Massine's contribution was, unhappily, null and void. When one has to fall back for audience reaction on a pantomime horse—albeit a singularly charming one, with an Afro-Cubist head and an undisciplined habit of rearing on its hind legs—things have come, choreographically speaking, to a pretty pass. In fact *Parade* was probably never much good as a ballet. It was a manifesto of Cubism, an attempt to shock the

audience (successful, one must add), and Cocteau's response to
Diaghilev's famous '*Etonne-moi*'. One was intensely grateful
to have been given the opportunity to see it, but one began to
see why Diaghilev did not revive it a great deal (apart from
the fact that it acquired the same ill-fated atmosphere that
Macbeth possesses—and Diaghilev was a very superstitious man).

There remains the score. This is divided as follows: *Choral*;
Prélude du rideau rouge; *Prestidigitateur chinois*; *Petite fille américaine*; *Acrobates*; *Final—Suite au prélude du rideau rouge*. After
the introductory *Choral* the score proceeds in segments, without
development, accommodating *chinoiserie*, circus elements and a
Ragtime du pâquebot for the Little American Girl, as well as a
typewriter, pistol shots and a foghorn. There were to have
been many more added noises, if Cocteau had got his way,
including shouts of gibberish by the Managers (presumably
'authentic circus gibberish' on the lines of the 'authentic
Frontier gibberish' in *Blazing Saddles*), sirens, aeroplane
noises, dynamos. But in the event most of these were suppressed, to Cocteau's dissatisfaction. The typewriter did
however get a credit in the programme ('by Underwood').
Satie said, with what Cocteau called modesty, and I should
call coolness, that he had 'composed a background to certain
noises that Cocteau considered necessary to define the atmosphere of his characters'. We shall never know what Satie
thought of the final result, though we do know that towards
the end of the creative process he was more drawn to Picasso's
ideas than to Cocteau's.

What of the music? How does it strike people who hear it?
To a greater degree than any other work of Satie, *Parade*
presents problems for the listener. Not that it is 'complex': on
the contrary, it is simple indeed, or so it seems. But its apparent
simplicity makes it all the more foxing.

It would be hard to find a listener who thought that the
Finale of Beethoven's *Choral Symphony* did not express joy, that
Chabrier's *Fête polonaise* did not express gaiety, that the
Abschied from *Das Lied von der Erde* was not intended to be
intensely sad. To take works by the composers under consideration, Milhaud's *Le Train bleu* and *Le Boeuf sur le Toit*
are clearly meant to be jolly. Poulenc's *Stabat Mater* is pre-
dominantly sad. None of these is a work that one can take two

ways. There is a different type of composition where there is an underlying sadness or nostalgia, sometimes only half perceived, under a surface joyousness; examples are Mozart's *Così fan tutte*, Debussy's *Ibéria*, Poulenc's *Les Biches*. Most people sense these undercurrents and agree that they are present.

Parade is not a bit like that. The programme of the Diaghilev season at the Alhambra Theatre in London in April 1919 called it 'a merry display'. Apollinaire, no fool, spoke of it as 'extremely clear, simple and expressive music which it is impossible not to recognise as the pure and transparent air of our France' (*Parade et l'esprit nouveau* in the Diaghilev Paris programme). Felix Aprahamian has spoken of the work's 'uncomplicated gaiety'. Rollo Myers has written that it has 'a kind of hallucinatory quality'. David Drew speaks of the violence underlying Satie's music and compares the atmosphere that *Parade* exhales to the empty, lonely, doomed feeling that one finds in the early paintings of Giorgio de Chirico.

Sauguet's *Les Forains*, a charming work which is clearly the offspring of *Parade* (and which its composer dedicated to Satie in homage to *Parade*) presents no problem: it offers the classical, even banal mixture of tears and cheers associated with the world of the circus. Not so *Parade*. It would probably be well to say that I belong firmly to what one might call the 'Drew' school: I never cease to be struck by the quite appalling feeling of loneliness *Parade* conveys and the cold controlled ferocity of some of its episodes. Those who would characterise it as light-hearted, frothy and Parisian seem to me to fall into the same category as a radio announcer I once heard introducing Ravel's *Scarbo* with the words 'See the merry little gnome . . .'

At all events *Parade* is of great historic importance: in its short timespan (it lasts hardly a quarter of an hour) it encompasses neoclassicism, jazz, America, the music-hall, the circus—all the characteristic obsessions of the 1920s.

Socrate, Satie's other masterpiece, is utterly different. And it had no influence. It had much prestige: Ned Rorem has written that 'all the 1920 Paris–New Yorkers had a copy, sacred as the Bible but infinitely rarer, just as Falla's *Harpsichord Concerto* is the golden calf of young South Americans'.

Socrate had indeed an immense reputation among professional musicians, but in its nature it could have no direct influence on their methods of work.

Satie had been approached by the members of a kind of salon in the studio of the painter Lejeune, at 6 rue Huyghens in Montparnasse: a salon run largely by the writer Blaise Cendrars in an effort to bring together the various artists of the 'new spirit' in music, writing and painting. Picasso, Matisse, Braque and Derain showed their pictures there, and from time to time music was performed. On 6 June, 1917, a fortnight after the premiere of *Parade*, Satie figured in a programme there alongside Georges Auric, then eighteen, Louis Durey and Honegger. Later on, Francis Poulenc, Germaine Tailleferre and Darius Milhaud, recently back from Brazil, joined the circle. Soon the concerts at 6 rue Huyghens grew very crowded, and so the singer Jane Bathori gave the musicians the opportunity of appearing at Jacques Copeau's Théâtre du Vieux-Colombier, which was nearby. When Copeau went to America in 1917 he had entrusted the actor Pierre Bertin with the task of arranging lectures and literary evenings at the theatre. The musicians gave their first concert there on 15 January, 1918. Among their associates were Cocteau, Valentine Hugo and not only Pierre Bertin but another actor, Marcel Herrand, who was to appear in Cocteau's plays in the future. The music critic Henri Collet christened the Auric–Poulenc–Milhaud–Honegger–Durey–Tailleferre group *Les Six*. This description arose out of an article in *Comoedia* (20 January, 1920), the first of two by Collet, and called *Les cinq Russes, les six Français et M. Erik Satie*. Satie preferred the name *Les Nouveaux Jeunes*.

It was Jane Bathori who suggested to the Princesse de Polignac that she should commission *Socrate* from Satie, and she who sang it first, with the composer at the piano, in her own house and in the salon of the Princesse, to whom the score had been dedicated. The piano version was a reduction: the work in its final version was scored for four sopranos (though, since they never sing together, it is feasible to use only one artist for the purpose), with a small orchestra composed of single woodwind, horn, trumpet, harp, timpani and strings. This was heard in public for the first time on 7 June, 1920, at the Salle Erard, with Marya Freund (famous for her performances of *Pierrot lunaire*) as singer and an orchestra under Félix Delgrange, a 'cellist who had been concerned in organising the concerts at the rue Huyghens. *Socrate* evoked giggling incomprehension.

There was much talk in the 1920s of a *style dépouillé* and of *musique dépouillée*—music 'stripped' down to its essentials—and no more extreme instance could be found than *Socrate*. There are three movements: *Portrait de Socrate; Bords de l'Ilissus;* and *Mort de Socrate*. In the first, whose text is drawn from Plato's *Symposium*, Alcibiades draws a verbal picture of Socrates; in the second Socrates and Phaedrus walk by the banks of the river Ilissus; in the third, the longest section, Phaedo tells the story of the death of Socrates. Throughout, the music pursues a superficially untroubled and unemphatic course, its main function, so it seems, to set in relief the delivery of the text in Victor Cousin's translation, which some find old-fashioned and somewhat stilted, but which Satie liked and which, to my ear, sounds well. It will be seen that the design of the music places great responsibility on the shoulders of the singers or singer; the vocal line does not require virtuosity, but it does require perfect intonation, perfect French, sensitivity to the sounds and meanings of words, and, in general, *discretion*. Satie's vocal line is so wedded to the natural rhythm and pace of the words that when he chooses to decorate a word or a syllable he achieves a very telling effect with slight means. For instance, when Alcibiades speaks in the first section of *la manie dansante des corybantes* the melodic line achieves with the simplest of means a feeling of strangeness and exoticism, simply by lingering on the final word with a descent of a fifth and another of a fourth. Likewise, at the very end of the final section, the rise (again of a fourth) at the words *le plus juste et le meilleur de tous les hommes* creates an emotional effect out of all proportion to the simplicity of the technical device Satie uses. The slightest vocal gesture tells. All in all, *Mort de Socrate* is an extraordinary piece of writing, the more so when one considers what a late romantic composer would have been likely to make of a description of the enforced death of one of the greatest men who ever lived. For those attuned to its style the final section of *Socrate* can be almost unbearably painful and distressing; yet the music never for an instant 'tugs at the heartstrings', it resists the temptation to emotionalise, and indeed, after the last words have been sung, it becomes nothing more than a bare repetition of alternating chords of the fifth before stopping, abruptly and without resolution.

It goes without saying that *Socrate* is a very difficult work to perform: not technically, but stylistically. This is true of all Satie; the notes are easy enough, as a rule, but the style is hard to catch. In the profusion of recordings of his music that have appeared in recent years only a very few are successful in this respect. *Socrate* has suffered more than any of them from singers with an imperfect command of French and conductors determined to import an element of *rubato* where little or none is required. It is not without significance that the finest performance of the work I have heard, with Anne Laloë as soloist, was directed by Henri Sauguet, no great conductor but a musician with a veneration for Satie, whose friend he was, and a complete understanding of his style.

Some other works by Satie, which show a closer connection with popular music, will be considered later.

Three pieces on which Stravinsky had worked during his sojourn in Switzerland during the 1914–18 War had to wait till it was over before they were heard elsewhere. These were *L'Histoire du soldat*, *Le Renard* and *Les Noces*. The second and third eventually entered the Diaghilev repertory, but Diaghilev showed no interest in staging the first. Stravinsky had written it in 1917–18 and it was first performed at the Théâtre de Lausanne on 27 September, 1918, with Georges and Ludmilla Pitoëff taking part and Ernest Ansermet conducting. The score of this tale of a soldier, the Devil and a magic violin has neoclassic elements, and much use is made of a chorale which is a distortion of *Ein feste Burg*. There are also features deriving from Stravinsky's study of the popular music which Ansermet had brought back from the U.S. The princess awakens to the strains of a *Ragtime* of sorts, though Stravinsky's treatment of ragtime components would have seemed very strange to American popular musicians of the period. There are also elements of Spanish march and pasodoble, while the use of the percussion (notably in the *Marche triomphale* of the Devil at the end) is more African than negro-American in feeling. With the merest handful of instruments (violin,

double-bass, clarinet, bassoon, trombone, cornet and percussion) Stravinsky demonstrated his supreme ability to create
rhythmic tension and vitality when such qualities were needed.
The work has great power and is arguably a masterpiece.

Le Renard, histoire burlesque chantée et jouée, is a shorter and
slighter work, though it packs a considerable punch. Diaghilev
took it into his repertory on 18 May, 1922 (the first performance
was at the Paris Opéra, with choreography by Nijinska and
designs by Larionov), and revived it with fresh choreography
by Serge Lifar in 1929. Ansermet conducted the first staged
performance. The work is written for a solo quartet of two
tenors, baritone and bass, with a small instrumental group
composed of flute, clarinet, bassoon, two horns, trumpet,
percussion and string quartet, and a very prominent part for
the cimbálom. The work—a tale of a predatory fox and his
untimely end—is extremely Russian in feeling. No one has
ever succeeded in staging it satisfactorily (the singers are
normally placed in the pit while dancers mime the parts of
the animals), and the effect in the concert hall is inclined to be
slightly risible, with the animal sounds and the final (and
extremely exciting) *pribaoutki* or Russian nonsense words being
sung by gentlemen in full evening dress (the same problem
arises with the cats' duet in concert performances of Ravel's
L'Enfant et les sortilèges).

During the 1920s Stravinsky pursued in the main his own
version of neoclassicism, with such works as the *Piano Concerto*,
the *Capriccio*, the short opera *Mavra* with a text by Boris
Kochno (Opéra, 3 June, 1922, with sets by Léopold Survage),
the opera-oratorio *Oedipus Rex* on a Latin text, and the ballet
Apollon musagète, whose music contains more than an echo of
Tchaikovsky. This last work was begun in July, 1927, at Nice,
and finished early the following year. It was written to a
commission from Mrs Elizabeth Sprague Coolidge, and first
danced in Washington, on 27 April, 1928, with choreography
by Adolphe Bolm. Balanchine's version, one of his early
masterpieces, was presented by Diaghilev at the Théâtre Sarah
Bernhardt in Paris on the following 12 June, with the composer
in the pit, a set by the primitive painter André Bauchant, and
costumes by Chanel. But the work of Stravinsky's which made
a greater impact than any of these was *Les Noces*.

Stravinsky had conceived the idea of a ballet on the theme of a Russian village wedding in 1914, at the same time that Cocteau was trying to interest him in *David*. But while *Parade*, the final version of *David*, saw the light in 1917, it took nearly ten years before Stravinsky's own project came before the public. He had discussed it with the designer Nathalie Gontcharova after the premiere of *Le Coq d'Or*, for the sets and costumes of which she had been responsible. It will be remembered that this was a highly elaborate and expensive production of Rimsky-Korsakov's work as an opera-ballet, with a double cast of singers and dancers, and the chorus ranged in tiers at the sides of the stage. Gontcharova's very colourful sets and costumes were based on Russian peasant motifs. Stravinsky said that in his opinion designs in similar style would be suitable for the project which he had in mind.

Gontcharova did not begin her work on the designs until early 1916. She followed Stravinsky's ideas, and at one stage produced designs, with which she was well pleased, for costumes in pastel colours embroidered with silver, pale gold, white and grey pearls and silk. Meanwhile, in Switzerland, Stravinsky was working on his music, and had completed the short score by 1917. He wrote that he played some of the music to Diaghilev, who 'wept and said it was the most beautiful and purely Russian creation of our Ballet. I think he did love *Les Noces* more than any other work of mine. That is why it is dedicated to him.'

Stravinsky contemplated various orchestral clothings for his ideas, and he is said at one time to have thought of using an orchestra of 150 players, larger even than that required for *Le Sacre du printemps*. It was only in early 1923 that he completed his final version, which is for vocal soloists, chorus, four pianos and a great deal of percussion. Gontcharova has written* that during the spring of that year Diaghilev sent for her and told her that the work was to be staged that season; the music was ready, and Nijinska was already rehearsing the dancers at Monte Carlo. The singers and the four pianos would be on stage. Gontcharova says that she outlined to Diaghilev at once her simple, final ideas about the design,

* Nathalie Gontcharova: The Creation of *Les Noces*, *Ballet*, September 1949.

and Diaghilev, to her astonishment, expressed no objection and made no criticism of any kind. If her memory serves her right, hers was an inspiration indeed. Indeed Diaghilev, normally very active in the preparation of the ballets he was to stage, seems to have played little part in the creation of this work. It is said that at the first rehearsal he saw he was so moved that he was unable to speak.

The story of the creation of these *scènes chorégraphiques russes avec chant et musique* is one of continual simplification and elimination. In this connection some words of the great designer Christian Bérard are relevant. Speaking of the art of stage design, he said:

> The finest *mises en scène* have been done by Meyerhold in Russia. They were so fine precisely because there was nothing there. It was an art of extraordinary allusive power. In Ostrovsky's *Forest* everything was suggested by a plank and three steps, and it was marvellous. Because this *nothing* is everything. And *everything is there* because *everything has been taken away*. Obviously, you can't make *anything* with nothing. You have to start by putting everything there and then take it away bit by bit.*

In the end Diaghilev placed two double pianos (Pleyela) in the pit, which he enlarged by taking out the first row of the stalls. The premiere was at the Théâtre du Gaieté-Lyrique on 13 June, 1923, with, as pianists, Edouard Flament, Auric, Marcelle Léon and Marcelle Meyer. When the work was first seen in London, at His Majesty's Theatre on 14 June, 1926, the pianists were four composers, taking part in the performance as a homage to Stravinsky. They were Auric once again, Poulenc, Vladimir Dukelsky and Vittorio Rieti. This charming gesture was repeated on a gramophone recording in the U.S., with Aaron Copland, Lukas Foss, Samuel Barber and Roger Sessions taking part (not, it is said, with great success, for the lack of expertise of some of the distinguished participants drove the master to the whisky bottle and at one point led him to attack a sofa with his fists. Lukas Foss found himself playing more and more, the others less and less.) When the Royal Ballet revived the work under the supervision

* *Graphis*, vol. 2, no. 15, May–June 1946.

of Nijinska on 23 March, 1966, the pianists were Richard
Rodney Bennett, John Gardner, Edmund Rubbra and
Malcolm Williamson.

This production was subsequently seen in the U.S., while
Jerome Robbins' very different version has been seen at Covent
Garden. Nijinska's is immensely superior. The Robbins
version has a Jewish feel about it: one expects Topol to appear
at any moment. No work could be less Jewish than *Les Noces*.

The revival of the Nijinska version was truly—to use a
much-abused word—a revelation. As has been mentioned, in
the concert hall or on the air the work's chosen sound spectrum
can dull the ear. Its utter rightness became clear to me—and,
I suspect, to many others—on both seeing and hearing the
work in the theatre. Who could forget the explosion of the last
scene, when, as the lament of the mothers dies away amid a
murmuring on the pianos and an occasional soft single stroke
on the xylophone, the stage suddenly blazes with light and the
celebratory dances of the corps de ballet begin? Or the final
pages, when the Bride and Bridegroom have disappeared
into the bedroom and one of the male soloists sings the Bridegroom's words of love, which finally resolve into a simple
motive on bells and pianos? One of Stravinsky's greatest
strengths is his sense of ritual. Every work, in a sense, becomes a
rite. Even the *Lanterloo* procession in *The Rake's Progress*, where
Mother Goose and Tom are led to bed, has this extraordinary
feeling. *Les Noces* is one of the century's incontrovertible
masterpieces. It is also the perfect answer to those who say
that great art cannot be accomplished through the medium of
the ballet.

5

The Music-hall and the Circus

*Assez de nuages, de vagues, d'aquariums, d'ondines et de parfums la
nuit; il nous faut une musique sur la terre, une musique de tous les
jours.*   —Jean Cocteau, *Le Coq et l'arlequin*

The music-hall and the circus, so beloved of the French
composers of the 1920s, were not new subjects for art: there
had, after all, been the paintings of Dégas and Toulouse-
Lautrec and the work of Picasso's Harlequin Period. But a
painter can use any subject at all for his work without thereby
pre-determining the style in which he is to paint. This is not
true of a musician. If a composer opts to introduce into his
work elements suggestive of the kind of music to be heard in
the music-hall or at the circus, or if he decides to base a whole
work on such elements, there are definite consequences for the
form and substance of his work. What results is likely to be
popular in style, melodic, somewhat square-cut; the dangers
are brashness and vulgarity, qualities easy to recognise but
hard to define and impossible to analyse. In any case, to some
of the composers of the 1920s, it seemed that refinement had
gone too far with Debussy and Ravel and that it was time to
return, in Cocteau's words, to 'une musique de tous les jours'.

The pioneer in this area, as in so many others, was Satie.
During his days as a Montmartre café pianist he had written
songs like *Je te veux* and *Tendrement* for the singer Paulette
Darty, and his song *La Diva de l'Empire* (written around 1900)
contains suggestions of ragtime. In the spring of 1899 he
composed *Jack in the Box*, a suite of three movements intended
as accompaniment to a pantomime on a scenario by Satie's
friend Jules Depaquit, to be presented at the Comédie parisienne. In fact it was never performed. Satie said of it that 'it
consoles me a little; it will be my rude gesture to the evil men
inhabiting our world'. He then proceeded to lose the score
and it was discovered after his death, in 1925, behind a piano
in his miserable lodgings at Arcueil. The marionette opera

Geneviève de Brabant turned up at the same time. Milhaud orchestrated *Jack in the Box* and Diaghilev presented it as a ballet at the Théâtre Sarah Bernhardt on 3 June, 1926. The set, with its cut-out cardboard clouds, was by Derain, the choreography by Balanchine, and the work mainly designed as a vehicle for the virtuosity of Idzikovsky, who was supported by Danilova, Doubrovska and Tchernicheva. The little work is quite astonishing in the way that it demonstrates how Satie foreshadowed and anticipated much that was to come in music. Its inspiration is clearly the music-hall, but its freshness of melodic and especially of harmonic invention prevents it from becoming banal at any point, a danger not always avoided by Satie's disciples.

In *Le Piège de Méduse*, written in 1913, Satie not only once again foreshadowed the forthcoming interest in the music-hall: he anticipated Dada, the movement which is usually thought to have been 'invented' officially by Tristan Tzara at Zurich in February, 1916. Satie's description of this piece is: *comédie en un acte de M. Erik Satie (avec musique du même monsieur).* The characters in the little play include the Baron Méduse, his *fille de lait* (!) Frisette, her lover Astolfo and the Baron's manservant Polycarpe. There is also Jonas, a stuffed monkey, who dances between the scenes. The music is scored for clarinet, trumpet, trombone, violin, 'cello, double-bass and percussion. The work was not staged until Pierre Bertin produced it on 23 May, 1921, as part of an evening of *avant-garde* comedy which also included Cocteau's *Le Gendarme incompris*.

In the catalogue of innovations and anticipations for which Satie was responsible or with which he was associated mention should also be made of the *Cinq grimaces pour un songe d'une nuit d'été*. During the 1914–18 War Cocteau conceived the idea of making a version of *A Midsummer Night's Dream* for playing in a circus ring (the Cirque Médrano) by clowns (the Fratellinis, who later took part in *Le Boeuf sur le Toit*). Cocteau made a version of the play for this purpose (it appears to have been lost), and succeeded in interesting the impresario Gabriel Astruc in the project. Satie wrote the *Cinq grimaces* for this production, which never materialised, but whose idea interestingly anticipates Peter Brook's treatment of the play over fifty years later.

Satie's work between the composition of *Parade* and *Socrate* and his death on 1 July, 1925, bore more relation to the earlier works just discussed than to his two masterpieces. In 1920 he composed, for the dancer Mlle Caryathis, then appearing at the Comédie des Champs-Elysées and later the wife of the writer Marcel Jouhandeau, a suite for small theatre orchestra with pianist-conductor, which he called *La Belle Excentrique*. This is unambiguously cheerful, indeed somewhat raucous, and while it lacks the subtlety of *Jack in the Box* it has considerable verve. After a so-called *Grande ritournelle*, there is a *Marche Franco-lunaire*, a *Valse du mystérieux baiser dans l'oeil* and a final *Can-can grand-mondain*.

Between 1920 and 1925 Satie composed two more ballets, neither of the calibre of *Parade* but both of considerable interest and attraction. The first, *Les Aventures de Mercure*, arose out of the activities of Count Etienne de Beaumont. Beaumont, who was both rich and cultivated, commissioned private entertainments for the parties which he gave in the garden of his Paris hotel. These acquired so distinguished an artistic reputation that he was persuaded to transfer them to a theatre and open them to the public. The result was the *Soirées de Paris*, a season of seven weeks at the Théâtre de la Cigale in 1924, and another season of similar length the following year. Plays were presented as well as ballets. They included Tristan Tzara's *Mouchoir de nuages* and Cocteau's version of *Romeo and Juliet*, which he called a *prétexte à mise en scène en cinq actes et 23 tableaux d'après William Shakespeare* (2 June, 1924). Jean Hugo dressed the actors in black tights which tended to merge them with the black curtains that formed the scenery, only a splash of colour on the costumes defining their silhouettes, while huge white collars framed their faces. The brilliant young conductor and composer Roger Desormière (a member, with Sauguet, Maxime Jacob and Henri Clicquet-Pleyel, of the so-called *Ecole d'Arcueil*, who took this name in homage to Satie) composed music 'after English popular airs'. Among the ballets given were the original versions of *Scuola di ballo*, *Gaîté parisienne* and *Le Beau Danube* (then called *Le Beau Danube bleu*), Sauguet's *Les Roses* with designs by Marie Laurencin, Milhaud's *Salade* and *Mercure*.

Mercure was given the untranslatable subtitle *poses plastiques en trois tableaux* and at the opening night (15 June, 1924), which was somewhat riotous, Picasso's striking designs slightly eclipsed both Satie's music and Massine's choreography. Satie's *Overture* is in what might be called his music-hall vein, but much of the rest of the music is very classical in feeling, and, as is well known, he represented *Chaos* by simply combining two of the earlier movements, not, it should be added, with a harshly dissonant effect: he obtained the result he wanted through the mutual incongruity of the two movements thus combined. Diaghilev took *Mercure* into his repertory four years later (2 June, 1927), but it was never one of his more popular ballets.

Satie's second ballet in 1924, *Relâche*, was produced by the Swedish Ballet; it was, in fact, their last creation. Between the first performance of *Mercure* in June and that of *Relâche* in the winter André Breton had published his Surrealist Manifesto, and the first number of *La Révolution surréaliste* appeared on 1 December. There was much interest at the time in the machine. Jane Heap held a Machine-Age exhibition at the Little Review Gallery in Fifth Avenue, New York. Léger was painting mechanistic pictures. The expatriate American composer George Antheil wrote a *Ballet mécanique*, and Léger collaborated with the American cameraman Dudley Murphy in producing a film to accompany Antheil's music. Honegger's once-famous symphonic movement *Pacific 231* had its first performance under Koussevitzsky on 8 May, 1924.

Satie's collaborator in *Relâche* was the artist Francis Picabia, whose work reflected both Dada and surrealism, and the whole enterprise was deliberately designed to provoke. Borlin was in charge of the choreography, but this was swamped by the fanciful designing which included, for instance, a set composed entirely of gramophone records. There was no decipherable plot. The ballet was described as a *ballet instantanéiste en deux actes, un entr'acte cinématographique, et 'la queue du chien'* (the 'dog's tail' being a *petite danse finale* or *chanson mimée*). The description was clearly intended to confuse the public, and it did. René Clair was responsible for the filmed entr'acte, in which Satie and others were seen firing cannon and crawling about on the roof of Notre Dame. For this entr'acte Satie composed a score made up of constantly repeated musical phrases, placed side by side and bearing no apparent relation to the images of the film. This has been recorded, but it makes intolerable listening on its own. Indeed it was never intended to be listened to as such, any more than the so-called *Musique d'ameublement* Satie had composed four years earlier (scoring it for piano, three clarinets and bass trombone). It may be recalled that Satie had intended this to be played during the interval of a theatrical performance and the last thing he wished was that anyone should actually listen to it. When people started to do so, the composer moved from group to group, urging them to talk.

Satie's score for the ballet *Relâche* itself, as opposed to the film, is agreeable and attractive, making use of French popular songs from time to time, notably *Cadet Roussel*, but once again the spectacular and surprising nature of the designing tended to overshadow not only the choreography but the music, which was conducted by Roger Desormière. *Relâche* is the French equivalent of 'Theatre closed' or '*Oggi riposo*', but the joke backfired, for when the audience arrived for the first performance they did indeed find the Théâtre des Champs-Elysées closed: the performance had been postponed. When the first performance finally took place, on 29 November, the audience was bemused and irritated and there was a good deal of hostility at the end, when Picabia and Satie drove on to the stage in a little car.

This was Satie's last work for the theatre. By this time he was somewhat estranged from Cocteau, who had, Satie thought, moved to the right, artistically speaking. Under the influence of the young Raymond Radiguet, Cocteau's verse had become for the time being classical in form and feeling, the most notable instance being the collection *Plain-chant*, composed for the most part of love poems to Radiguet. The surrealists, especially Breton, disliked and distrusted Cocteau, and Satie now tended to share their view of him.

Among his manifold activities at this time Cocteau had been instrumental in the creation of two spectacles which showed very strongly the influence of the music-hall. These were *Le Boeuf sur le Toit* and *Les Mariés de la Tour Eiffel*.

Darius Milhaud wrote the music for the first of these

163699

enterprises in Paris in 1919. He called it a *Cinéma-symphonie* and thought that its character would make it suitable, perhaps, as accompaniment for a Charlie Chaplin film. There appears to be some argument as to whether the title was that of a Brazilian bar or a Brazilian popular song. At all events Milhaud 'assembled a few popular melodies, tangos, maxixes, sambas and even a Portuguese fado, and transcribed them with a rondo-like theme recurring between each successive pair'. The refrain passes through twelve major keys and is heard twelve times in the main section and thrice in the coda. As Milhaud stated, the music has Latin American constituents, but there are also traces of jazz and much that suggests the music-hall. Both Constant Lambert and David Drew have thought ill of the work, but it is pleasant enough in an unpretentious way and contains a number of happy melodic inventions.

At this point the *Six*'s 'manager', Cocteau, took the idea over. He saw it as a stage spectacle and it was eventually presented as such at a private performance at the Comédie des Champs-Elysées on 21 February, 1920. Poulenc's Cocteau song cycle *Cocardes* and Georges Auric's foxtrot *Adieu, New York* also figured in the programme. The main work was given a subtitle and a description, so that it now became *Le Boeuf sur le Toit ou The Nothing Doing Bar, farce imaginée et réglée par Jean Cocteau*.

An artist called Guy-Paul Fauconnet had designed the costumes, which included giant heads for the characters, but before he could proceed to the sets he was asphyxiated by the stove in his studio and Raoul Dufy was brought in to complete his work. Vladimir Golschmann conducted the orchestra. As the description stated, Cocteau himself staged the piece, with a cast from the Cirque Médrano including some of the Fratellini family of clowns to mime the characters, who included a barman, a negro boxer, a bookmaker and a policeman.

The scene was a bar in America during Prohibition (which had been introduced the year before and continued in force until 1933). All the movements of the characters were slowed down, as in a film running at slow motion. Various figures come and go. The boxer's cigar is drawing badly, and at his request the barman shoots the end off with a revolver. Ladies of the town chat to the negro boxer. Another negro, a billiard-player, appears and disappears. A police whistle is heard. At once the barman hides the drinks and puts up a sign saying 'Only milk served here'. The policeman tastes the milk suspiciously, but is reassured. '*Influencé par l'esprit bucolique, il danse un ballet aimable*', says Cocteau's published scenario (these always make good reading). However the barman suddenly presses a lever and an electric fan descends and decapitates the policeman. But no one turns a hair: '*rien n'étonne les noctam-bules.*' One of the women, emulating Salome, dances with the giant head, 'shaking it like a cocktail'. Finally, when all but the barman have left, he puts the pieces of the policeman to-gether again and presents him with a bill three yards long. This piece of agreeable buffoonery was successful enough to be taken to London, where it was seen in July at the Coliseum.

Les Mariés de la Tour Eiffel, spectacle de Jean Cocteau, was an altogether more ambitious affair. Cocteau originally asked Georges Auric to provide all the music for his story of a wedding party on the Eiffel Tower, but Auric proved too busy to undertake the whole score in time for the premiere. Cocteau then decided that it should be a collaborative effort for all of *Les Six*. This was not quite what happened, since Louis Durey was out of sympathy with the idea and played no part in it. Indeed, he very shortly drifted away from the rest of the group. Thus the only enterprise in which all six composers took part was the *Album des Six* of 1920.

For some considerable time it was thought that the score of *Les Mariés* had been lost. Indeed, when the BBC presented a radio performance in the early days of its 'Third Programme' they were obliged to look elsewhere for suitable music, and eventually used Ibert's *Divertissement*, a popular but coarse piece. Then, in 1956, the score was rediscovered by Cocteau in the archives of the Dance Museum at Stockholm, to which Rolf de Maré had left much material associated with the Swedish Ballet. The allocation of responsibility for the move-ments was as follows:

Ouverture: le 14 juillet	Auric
Marche nuptiale	Milhaud

Discours du général	Poulenc
La baigneuse de Trouville	Poulenc
La massacre (fugue)	Milhaud
Valse des dépêches	Tailleferre
Marche funèbre	Honegger
Quadrille	Tailleferre
Three Ritournelles	Auric
Sortie de la noce	Milhaud

Given the very real differences in style between the members of the group, the mix worked extraordinarily well. Speaking of these differences, Milhaud once said that 'Auric and Poulenc were drawn to Cocteau's ideas, Honegger to German romanticism, myself to Mediterranean lyricism'. Poulenc said similar things: 'What could be more different than the music of Honegger and that of Auric? Milhaud admired Magnard, while I did not; neither of us liked Florent Schmitt, whom Honegger respected; and by contrast Arthur (Honegger), deep down inside himself, despised Satie, whom Auric, Milhaud and I adored.' It was perhaps as well that Honegger was allotted the Funeral March, which it is possible to take quite seriously until you spot a slowed-down version of the famous waltz from *Faust*. Many of the audiences at the time missed this allusion and thought that Honegger was showing commendable seriousness, lacking in his fellow-composers.

For the first performance by the Swedish Ballet at the Théâtre des Champs-Elysées on 18 June, 1921, Irène Lagut designed a charming set which represented a view of Paris as seen from the Eiffel Tower, while Jean Hugo's costumes, which included masks for all the characters, rediscovered the charm and elegance of the *belle époque*, a period then regarded as absurd and outmoded. Inghelbrecht conducted, and the 'phonos'—speakers dressed as gramophones—were 'played' by the *Six's* actor friends Pierre Bertin and Marcel Herrand. They were the only participants who spoke, and they were directed to do so very loud and very fast, pronouncing each syllable as distinctly as possible. Borlin was credited with the choreography, but given the nature of the undertaking he could do little more than carry out the instructions of the mind behind the whole spectacle: Cocteau.

Inevitably, *Les Mariés* was seen as frivolous, and it is indeed very funny at times. Yet no less a playwright than Jean Anouilh has referred to it as a perfect example of what Cocteau called his *poésie de théâtre*. *Les Mariés* was a serious attempt to use the commonplace events of ordinary daily life as materials for art and poetry by stripping them (that word again) of heir apparent banality. As such it could be regarded as a precursor, to some degree, of Pop Art.

It is the 14th of July and we are on the first platform of the Eiffel Tower. An ostrich appears, stalked by a sportsman intent on shooting it. But he misses and bags, instead, a large blue telegram, which falls to the ground. The director of the Tower appears, incensed at this crime. Meanwhile a photographer comes on to the scene, seeking the ostrich. That morning, when photographing a female client, he had assured her that as usual a bird would emerge ¦from his apparatus. But this time, in place of the usual small bird, an ostrich came out and proceeded to run away. He is now in hot pursuit of it so that he can persuade it to re-enter the camera. The director reads the telegram: it is a request to him to reserve a table for luncheon. A wedding party is on its way. But, says Phono One, it is a dead telegram. Precisely so, replies Phono Two: it is because it is dead that everyone can understand it.

To the strains of the *Marche nuptiale* the wedding party appears, each member announced by the Phonos. The bride is as sweet as a lamb, the father-in-law is as rich as Croesus, the General is as stupid as a goose, the bridesmaids are as fresh as roses. They sit down at table, on one side only, Phono 2 explains, so that the public can see them all properly. The General rises to speak: his gesticulations are accompanied by Poulenc's raucous *Discours*, whose music suggests military bands and fairs. The General continues by boring the company with an account of the phenomenon of the mirage, which he had experienced in Africa while eating alfresco with the Duc d'Aumale. Mirages, it seems, are very frequent on the Eiffel Tower. Sure enough, one appears: a female cyclist who is in reality on her way to Chatou. Unperturbed, the General assures her that she is indeed on the right road.

It is time for the group photograph. Unfortunately, as the photographer pronounces the fatal words *Un oiseau va sortir*,

there emerges not a small bird, not even an ostrich, but a
bathing-belle from Trouville. Her dance is, happily, a great
success. Poulenc's piece echoes the music of the *belle époque*,
as do the costumes of the characters. The baffled photographer
decides to let the wedding party think that he has arranged
this entertainment specially for their pleasure. '*Puisque ces
mystères me dépassent,*' he says (Phono One speaking on his behalf),
'*feignons d'en être l'organisateur.*' Fear in his heart, he tries again.
This time a child emerges, to be greeted with enthusiasm by
the family. The infant is hailed as the image of his father, of
his mother, of his grandmother, of his grandfather. He will
grow up to be a captain, an architect, a boxer, a poet, the
President of the Republic, *un beau petit mort pour la prochaine
guerre* (one of the text's occasional sardonic touches). But he
bombards the wedding group and 'massacres' them. However,
they recover in time for the Waltz of the Telegrams, the most
beautiful of whom is announced as the wireless telegraph, just
arrived from New York.

A further attempt is made to take a photograph. This time
it is to be of the General pretending to read the child something
by Jules Verne. This time a lion comes out of the camera.
The General, confident that this is another mirage, stands his
ground, only to learn that he is wrong. It is a real lion. General
and lion disappear underneath the table, from beneath which,
after a moment, the beast emerges with one of the General's
boots in its mouth. It re-enters the camera. A funeral march is
played. The father-in-law pronounces the funeral oration,
but refuses to bid the General adieu: it should be *au revoir*
merely, for his type will perpetuate itself as long as there are
men on earth. Gloom does not prevail for long, since the Band
of the *Garde Républicaine* is on hand to play Mlle Tailleferre's
Quadrille, with its traditional movements of *Pantalon*, *Eté*,
Poule, *Pastourelle* and *Final*. The photographer is offered
champagne. The child wants to feed the Eiffel Tower, but is
told sharply that it is fed only at certain times, and he may not.
To the photographer's delight, his ostrich reappears, and he
manages to entice it back into the camera before the pursuing
stalker can shoot it. The wedding party 'freezes', and is sold
for an enormous sum by a dealer in modern pictures. It is
God's most recent work; God, naturally, does not sign. At

last all is resolved. The camera disgorges the General, somewhat pale and short of one boot. The photographer manages a
successful photograph (a dove flies out), the wedding party
leaves, the Eiffel Tower closes for the day.

Les Mariés de la Tour Eiffel is a highly typical product of the
1920s. We are unlikely to see it recreated on the stage, but the
work has fortunately been recorded, under Milhaud. It remains
as fresh and amusing as when it was conceived, and it is not
without importance. Text and music have wit and gaiety,
but Cocteau, unlike Picabia, was a disciplined artist, and the
whole enterprise is under complete control. The concept (as
opposed to the music) of *Relâche* has dated; that of *Les Mariés*
has not.

Poulenc's two pieces for *Les Mariés* are among the most
amusing in the score. Another work of his, though not written
for the stage, relates so closely to the music-hall aesthetic that
it merits mention at this point. This was *Le Bal masqué*, which
he described as a '*cantate profane pour baryton et orchestre de
chambre sur des poèmes de Max Jacob*'. There is a prominent piano
part, and the other instruments used are oboe, clarinet,
bassoon, cornet, violin, 'cello and percussion. Poulenc wrote
the work in 1932 to a commission from the Noailles, and it was
first given on 20 April that year at Hyères, near Toulon, where
the Noailles had a country house. The soloist was Gilbert
Moryn, Poulenc played the piano, and Desormière conducted.
This was one of the performances during the Hyères Festival,
an event sponsored by the Noailles and for which a distinguished
group assembled, including, apart from those already mentioned, Georges and Nora Auric, Igor Markevitch, Boris
Kochno, Bérard, Giacometti and Luis Buñuel.

David Drew has written sharply of *Le Bal masqué*, using the
words 'infantile triviality'. I think that he has missed the point.
The music has wit, and so have the words, which Poulenc
drew from the collection of poems which Max Jacob called
Le Laboratoire central. Jacob was a Jewish convert to Roman
Catholicism, who alternated periods of theatrical but perfectly genuine devoutness with indulgence in the sins of the
flesh, which for him took the form of ether and boys. He
perished at the hands of the Nazis. His poems have at times
something of the same atmosphere as Edith Sitwell's early,

better work, though the resemblance should not be pushed too far. Poulenc chose poems from the collection which reminded him of the 'characters' he had observed during the summer holidays of his youth, mentioned already in connection with the *Concert champêtre*. He called the work 'a sort of *Carnaval nogentais*, with sketches of several monsters seen in my childhood along the banks of the Marne'. The *Préambule et air de bravoure* set the tone at once. Jacob's poem includes such puns as

> *Monsieur le Comte d'Artois*
> *Est monté sur le toit*
> *Faire un compte d'ardoises . . .*

After an instrumental *Intermède* there is a portrait, affectionately mocking yet sentimental, of one of the 'monsters', Malvina, whom one could pay court to only in a top hat. The closing words—'*Malvina, ô fantôme, que Dieu te garde*'—are set to a beautiful, swooning, waltz-like phrase. An instrumental *Bagatelle* precedes the last two songs, a rather sinister portrait of a blind woman, *La Dame aveugle*, and an exuberant finale which Poulenc intended as a portrait of Jacob himself as Poulenc knew him when he lived on rue Gabrielle in Montmartre in 1920.

Performed with the verve and wit that Poulenc and Bernac brought to it, the work had irresistible *entrain*. It would not translate at all, any more than, for instance, one could perform *Façade* in French or German.

Three other minor but interesting stage works found their inspiration in the music-hall and the circus. One of these was the ballet *Impressions de Music-Hall* by the conductor and composer Gabriel Pierné, presented with choreography by Nijinska at the Opéra in 1927 (8 April) and including numbers intended to represent such famous figures of the time as the Dolly Sisters and the Fratellinis.

Three years later, C. B. Cochran's *Revue of 1930* at the London Pavilion contained a short ballet called *Luna Park*, with music by Lord Berners, choreography by Balanchine, and sets and costumes by Christopher Wood. Lifar and Nikitina headed the cast. The high standard of the contributors is an eloquent testimony to Cochran's pursuit of excellence. It should also be remembered that Diaghilev had died the year before and his artists and dancers were available, nay eager, for work. In theme, though not in style, the ballet owed something to *Petrushka*.

The scene is a freak pavilion in a circus. The freaks on show are a man with three heads, one with six arms, a one-legged ballerina and a three-legged man who juggles with billiard balls. After their performance, when the Showman has disappeared for a time, the freaks emerge. They are in fact normally constructed human beings. They decide to go out into the world, and leave the circus. When it is time for the second performance there is no one left to give it and the Showman retreats in confusion. Berners' score has charm and Wood's contribution was stylish.

The last distinguished creation of the type we have been discussing was Sauguet's ballet *Les Forains*, already mentioned (see page 39), one of the earliest creations of what was to become the *Ballets des Champs-Elysées*. It was first given at the Théâtre des Champs-Elysées on 2 March, 1945, with choreography by the young Roland Petit and sets and costumes by Bérard. Sauguet wrote the score in three weeks, drawing on memories of the fairs at his native Bordeaux in his youth. The score for this ballet about 'strolling players' ranges from the exuberance of the movement called *Le prestidigitateur* (The Conjurer) to the sadness of the *Entrée des forains* and their final *Quête et départ*, when, having given their performance, they can collect pitifully little money from the crowd.

No one could claim that the score approaches the level of *Parade*, but the little ballet was, in its day, a masterpiece. I say *was* because it has now disappeared from the repertory of any company and during its brief life, lasting perhaps ten years, standards of performance steadily deteriorated. At the beginning, however, it had great beauty. Bérard was heavily influenced by the Picasso of the Harlequin Period in much of his work, and this is the atmosphere which *Les Forains* exhaled. The music was a little more tender and a little less astringent than it might have been if it had been composed in the 1920s (though there is little astringency in Sauguet's score for *La Chatte*, given in 1927), and in that sense the ballet cannot be said to be '1920ish'; yet the nature of its conception and its revealing dedication to Satie point to the link that exists.

6

Hedonism

Pleasure   Sport
The Beach   Seaports   Sailors

Les hommes trouveront toujours que la chose la plus sérieuse de leur existence, c'est jouir.

—Flaubert

The 1920s were pleasure-loving times. Those who had emerged from the holocaust with their lives intact and with money to spend gave themselves up to enjoyment. This was particularly true of the young: a certain justifiable cynicism and the feeling of having been spared by disaster combined to lead them to fling themselves with zest into the business of living. That there was a very grim side to the 1920s is not to be denied, but if one was young and comparatively well-off it was an agreeable time in which to live. This hedonistic approach found a ready reflection in the arts, and nowhere more than in certain French musical and theatrical works of the period, foremost among them the ballet *Les Biches*.

It is sad that Francis Poulenc should have written only three ballets, *Les Biches*, the *Aubade* of 1929 and the much later La Fontaine ballet *Les Animaux modèles* (1942). This was in sharp contrast with the extreme productivity of Milhaud, Auric and Sauguet in the balletic field. However each of Poulenc's trio of ballets is a work of great distinction, which is certainly not true of every work by the other three composers. Poulenc was himself the author of his ballet libretti, though in the case of his first work Diaghilev had asked him to write an atmospheric ballet on the lines of *Les Sylphides* and in the spirit of the *fêtes-galantes*.

For this, his first work on a large scale, Poulenc chose to use an orchestra of normal size and a small chorus, who sing in only three of the movements, the two *Chansons dansées* and the

movement called *Jeu*. The work was created at Monte Carlo
on 6 January, 1924, with choreography by Nijinska and sets
and costumes by Marie Laurencin. Edouard Flament conducted. At the first Paris performance (26 May, Théâtre des
Champs-Elysées) the conductor was André Messager and the
chef des choeurs was a comparatively unknown young man
called Victor de Sabata. In the original cast, the three men
were danced by Wilzak, Woizikovsky and Kremnew; Vera
Nemtchinova danced the *Adagietto*, Nijinska herself the
Rag-Mazurka; the *Petite chanson dansée* was performed by
Tchernicheva and Sokolova; and the corps de ballet of girls
included Doubrovska, Nikitina and Ninette de Valois. The
work was an immediate, great and lasting success.

It was revived between the wars by the Markova–Dolin
Company, after the 1939–45 War by the *Grand Ballet du
Marquis de Cuevas*, and, triumphantly, by the Royal Ballet on
2 December, 1964, at Covent Garden, with a cast headed by
Svetlana Beriosova, Georgina Parkinson, Merle Park, Maryon
Lane, David Blair, Keith Rosson and Robert Mead. For this
revival, which vindicated the work's status as a theatrical
masterpiece, Nijinska is said to have counselled the use of
Poulenc's 1947 re-orchestration, in which the choruses were
cued in in small notes, for use or disuse as required by the
management presenting the ballet. Thus audiences were
denied the opportunity of hearing the work as originally
conceived, with chorus, which was regrettable. But it would
be ungracious to carp at what was in almost every way a
loving, careful and highly successful recreation of the original.
There have been frequent performances of the revival since
1964, which makes it all the odder that James Harding, in his
agreeable book about Paris in the 1920s,* published in 1972,
should say that 'the steps the dancers followed are lost in time.
Though the music remains, we have to imagine the pinks and
pale blues of Marie Laurencin, and the blue velvet costume
Vera Nemtchinova wore as she danced the Adagietto'. Not a
bit of it: all one has to do is watch Covent Garden forward
programmes and take money to the box office.

During the *Overture* the curtain rises to reveal Marie
Laurencin's drop-curtain, with its charming reference to the

* James Harding: *The Ox on the Roof*, Macdonald, London, 1972.

title of the ballet, which can mean both 'hinds' or 'does', or alternatively 'darlings'. What it certainly does not mean is *The House Party*, which was the title given it by the Markova-Dolin Company, though Mr Peter Williams' perceptive remark that the ballet evokes 'the long, long house party of the twenties' is valid enough. When the *Overture* has finished the drop-curtain itself rises to show a large room, bare but for an enormous blue sofa. A small *corps de ballet* of girls have the first dance, a light-hearted *Rondeau*. Nijinska's choreography, notably the characteristic movements of the shoulders, is highly evocative of the coltish elegance fashionable at the time. A new and disturbing element is introduced with the appearance of three young men, dressed as athletes, during the *Chanson dansée*. To percussive music they strike 'he-man' poses, while in the nostalgic middle section the girls, interested, weave round them, the softness of their movements contrasting with the aggressive maleness of the men's. The words of this movement, like those of the other sung sections, were based by Poulenc on French popular songs of the folksong type, and bear no relation to the stage happenings. They begin with the question '*Qu'est-ce qu'Amour? Le connaîs-tu, Grégoire?*', which the published score helpfully translates as '*Say, what is love? Do you know him, McGregor?*', thus importing an inappropriately Scots element into the proceedings. During the famous and tender *Adagietto* which follows there appears a figure in blue velvet, one white-gloved hand raised to the cheek.* This character is danced by a woman and described frequently as 'The Girl in Blue', which is a mistake: the character is intended as a page-boy, a fact which imparts a distinctive flavour to later developments. The leader of the three athletes shows interest.

There follows the choral movement *Jeu*, a romp for the corps de ballet with, at least in the music, some oddly sinister undertones. There is a strange, serpentine passage in the middle of the movement. In the *Rag-Mazurka* an older woman, presumably the hostess of the party, if it is a party, dances with the two other men. There is a feeling that she is attempting to preserve her youth, which is beginning to vanish. She is clearly susceptible to the charms of her two young partners.

* See frontispiece. Makarova is the finest interpreter of this role in recent years.

The next two movements are both *pas de deux* of an equivocal nature: the first, the *Andantino*, is given to the principal athlete and the page-boy, the second, the *Petite chanson dansée*, a relentless march, to two girls, whose obvious affection for each other, somewhat stealthily expressed, suggests Albertine and a young friend at Balbec, in Proust's masterpiece. The finale, in which all join, has very much the feeling that everyone is almost certainly off to another party, probably on a yacht. I borrow this thought from Richard Buckle, who has quoted the late Lydia Sokolova as saying that as danced by the Royal Ballet the finale lacked this feeling, which it ought to have had. I must say that I did not feel anything was lacking.

In giving an account of the progress of the ballet one is in danger of over-emphasising the 'events' which may have taken place, and of making what is in fact subtle and ambiguous seem obvious or even crude. This impression could not be further from the truth: ambiguity is essential to the concept of this ballet. Poulenc said that 'in this ballet, as in certain of Watteau's pictures, there is an atmosphere of wantonness which you sense if you are corrupted, but which an innocent-minded girl would not be conscious of'.* In an article he has told us that one such simple creature told him that *Les Biches* was the modern *Les Sylphides*: the composer replied that he was glad that the ballet struck her that way.

Diana Menuhin (the former dancer Diana Gould) said to Richard Buckle that the work possessed 'that essential Diaghilev quality which was Russian passion filtered through French taste'. Mrs Menuhin, who took part in the Markova-Dolin revival, also said that the music itself told the dancers what they should do and how they should do it. 'Is there not,' she asked, 'mystery and humour and ambiguity and *chic* and mischief and great *maîtrise* in that score?' It is a score which contains many ingredients which might be thought ruinously disparate. Poulenc acknowledged debts—to *Mavra*, to *Pulcinella*, to a variation from *The Sleeping Princess* for the *Adagietto*. But there were many more, which formed the subject of the attack by Constant Lambert already mentioned. There is the sentimentality of the nineteenth century, the crispness of Mozart in his *galant* mood, suggestions of French folk song,

* Francis Poulenc on his ballets, *Ballet*, September 1946.

and the jazz element, which appears most notably in the *Rag-Mazurka*, whose strange title in itself crystallises the close juxtaposition of seemingly incongruous elements which is so pronounced a feature of the work. Yet Poulenc's personality is printed on every movement. It is a pity, incidentally, that the three sung movements are omitted from the usual Suite (the *Overture* is less of a loss), though an important and interesting French album issued in 1973 includes a recording of the entire work, with chorus. Its very subtle blend of gaiety and nostalgia contrasts strikingly with the next ballet I propose to discuss, Milhaud's *Le Train bleu*.

This work was written very quickly. Diaghilev went to see Milhaud while the latter was engaged in composing the ballet *Salade* for the *Soirées de Paris*. According to Milhaud, Diaghilev expressed the opinion that the *Soirées* had no future and it would be better for Milhaud to break with de Beaumont. It was certainly true that Diaghilev was alarmed at the competition from this new source, when he already had to deal with the modish Swedish Ballet as an alternative attraction to his own company. Milhaud replied that he had a contract with de Beaumont, which he intended to fulfil, but he had no objection to writing a ballet for Diaghilev as well. The Russian knew that Milhaud composed very fast, and he needed a ballet which would show off the young Anton Dolin during his forthcoming Paris season. Accordingly he commissioned a work, but stipulated that it should be something light, frivolous and in the style of Offenbach. Diaghilev did not care for Milhaud's more dissonant style. Cocteau, who was also concerned in the enterprise, asked for music 'of the kind you hear in the cinema when Mme Millerand visits a hospital' (Mme Millerand was the wife of the then French President). Milhaud set to work manfully and, having written *Salade* between 5 and 20 February, 1924, composed *Le Train bleu* between 15 February and 5 March. He dedicated the latter to Diaghilev. It was his first, and, as it turned out, only original ballet for the Russian company.

The new ballet, which was described as an *opérette dansée de Jean Cocteau*, was first seen at the Théâtre des Champs-Elysées on 20 June, 1924. The drop-curtain, with its heavy-breasted female figures, was by Picasso; the decor by the sculptor

Henri Laurens; the costumes—beach clothes and sports wear—by Chanel. The conductor was André Messager, sportingly consenting to direct an enterprise which was very much a send-up of the operettas of which he himself had composed so many. Milhaud himself took over in London. The scene was *une plage élégante* where the train of the title had already deposited its load of pleasure-seekers, made up of a chorus of *poules* and gigolos, and the principal characters—the woman tennis champion, the golfer and *Beau Gosse*, Dolin's role, in which he performed acrobatic feats that delighted the audience.

Unlike *Les Biches*, *Le Train bleu* has a definite and unambiguous plot, but it is extremely lightweight and not for a moment to be taken seriously. It concerns the sort of happenings which occur less on the beaches of real resorts than on the *plages* of countless musical comedies. The atmosphere is very much that of the number *Sur la plage* in Sandy Wilson's *The Boy Friend*. People flirt, bathe, lie about, take photographs of each other. An aeroplane passes, dropping handbills. This is during a scene which Cocteau called *Farce des cabines et scène de l'avion*. Cocteau wrote a fairly long scenario which contained detailed directions about the way the dancers were to move and the atmosphere they were to create. It contains such gems as:

> *Tout à coup la championne voit quelque chose qui l'effraye: c'est le joueur de golf, son flirt, qui approche . . .*
> *La baigneuse . . . montre sa figure et agite ses bras par les ouvertures de la cabine no. 2; le joueur de golf lui ouvre la porte.*
> *Flirt.*
> *Valse dansée . . .*

It is all very cheerful and agreeably silly. Milhaud's score too is lightweight and unsubtle. His work for de Beaumont, *Salade*, written at the same time, is more durable. Yet *Le Train bleu* must have been a charming entertainment, lively, amusing and up-to-the-minute. Chanel's costumes had much influence on fashion, as usual.

Le Train bleu was echoed by a later ballet, *Plage*, with a scenario by R. Kerdyk, music by Jean Françaix, choreography by Massine and designs by Dufy, which the de Basil Company presented on 18 April, 1933. This, however, was a much more straightforward 'beach ballet', as was the Balanchine–Robbins *Jones Beach* (1950). If my memory serves me right, the latter contained no attempt at characterisation. It was just another plotless Balanchine· ballet, which happened to be danced in swimming costumes. And 'costumes by Jantzen' lacks the ring of 'costumes by Chanel'. Still, they were no doubt provided free.

Honegger made his contributions to the interest in sport. These were, notably, the symphonic movement *Rugby*, written and performed in 1928, and the ballet *Skating Rink*, created by the Swedish Ballet on 20 January, 1922. This had a scenario by the Italian Canudo, sets and costumes by Fernand Léger and choreography by Borlin. The press wrote: 'English title, Swedish ballet, Italian scenario, Swiss music—a typically Parisian event. Everything went as smoothly as on roller-skates'. Diaghilev's death in 1929 is said to have spared the world a Hindemith ballet about bicycle racing, ominously called *Number 13*.

I have written elsewhere* about the interest in seaports, their life and their people, which, though not peculiar to the 1920s, was marked in the literature, art and music of the period. There are many instances: Constant Lambert's *Piano Concerto* and *Piano Sonata*, full of the atmosphere of Toulon and Marseille, and of course *The Rio Grande;* the paintings of the Hon. Stephen Tennant, who appears also to have projected or started, though not to have published, a book with the engaging title *Lascar: a Romance of the Maritime Boulevard;* the paintings of Edward Burra; Cocteau's auto-biographical (and mildly pornographic) novel *Le Livre blanc;* that brilliant and moving book *L'Age d'or* by Pierre Herbart, the friend of André Gide (though this was written much later); and many more. The fag-end (if one may so describe it) of this fascination with seaport life was Leonard Bernstein's highly successful ballet *Fancy Free* and its offshoots, the musical *On the Town* and the film of the same name; though, of course, the subject of sailors on shore has a whole literature of its own, ranging from the harmless cavortings of *Hit the Deck* through the sodomitical squalors of *Querelle de Brest* (though

* *Constant Lambert*, London, 1973.

this, we are told, is still art) to those slim volumes, on sale in Amsterdam shops, which depict in considerable detail what Nigel Dennis once called 'the revolting excesses of shore leave'.

Two musical examples are worth mention. One was light-hearted, the other so much the reverse that it hardly 'belongs' in this chapter at all. The first was called *Les Matelots*, the second *Le Pauvre Matelot*.

Les Matelots was Georges Auric's second ballet for Diaghilev (after *Les Fâcheux*, and before *La Pastorale*). It had choreography by Massine and sets by the young Spanish artist Pedro Pruna, very much in the manner of Picasso but prettied up: a kind of rococo to the other man's baroque. Kochno's scenario was set in a Mediterranean port: a sailor tests the virtue of his fiancée by going away and returning in disguise with two friends. Luckily, the girl resists their advances and all ends happily. The original leading dancers were Woizikovsky, Lifar and Slavinsky as the sailors, and Nem-tchinova as the girl. The ballet enjoyed immediate success (first performance: Théâtre de la Gaité-Lyrique, Paris, 17 June, 1925), and it lasted into the 1930s, when de Basil took it into his repertory. Auric's score was more popular in style than *Les Fâcheux*, as befitted the subject, and in the final scene he made use of some English sea shanties which the painter Nina Hamnett had whistled to the composer, anxious to finish his work but lacking for the moment melodic inspiration.

Le Pauvre Matelot is a very different affair. Jean Cocteau wrote the libretto of what he called a *complainte en trois actes*, and again thought of his favourite Auric as composer for it. But Auric was too busy once again, and the music was then entrusted to Milhaud. After a good deal of preliminary thought Milhaud set to work and completed the score in two weeks, between 26 August and 5 September, 1926. At that stage he scored it for an orchestra of normal size. Later, however, he made a version for thirteen instruments, which he came to prefer and which he used when he recorded the opera.

Milhaud's extreme productivity and the speed at which he habitually worked have led some to sneer at what they see as a lack of self-criticism and a willingness to accept low standards.

We have seen that, just as *Le Pauvre Matelot* was composed in two weeks, the two ballets of 1924 cost their creator only a month's work. But the fact that Milhaud worked so quickly and composed so much—and the opinion, widely held, that his output is extremely uneven—should not blind us to the fact that from time to time he could produce music of very high quality. *Le Pauvre Matelot* bears all the signs of having been written at white heat. Alas, after 1930, Milhaud seldom matched the best of his earlier work. Again and again, among his later pieces, one has the feeling that one note would do just as well as another.

The opera, which Milhaud dedicated to Henri Sauguet, was produced at the Opéra-comique on 12 December, 1927, in a double bill with, of all things, *Werther*. It was subsequently seen at the Théâtre de la Monnaie, in Brussels, rather more suitably accompanied by Honegger's *Antigone*, while in 1929 Alexander Zemlinsky conducted it in Berlin, with the beautiful Jarmila Novotna in the principal female role. It was a considerable success in Germany, and in fact is probably Milhaud's most frequently performed opera—partly because of its intrinsic quality, and partly because, unlike some of his later operas, such as *Christophe Colomb*, *Maximilien* and *David*, it requires only small forces: there are just four characters and no chorus.

The grim story was suggested to Cocteau by a news item which concerned the son of poor Rumanian parents who had gone as a boy to the U.S. and become rich. He decided to return, incognito, to see his parents. Taking him for a wealthy stranger, they robbed and killed him.

Cocteau varies the story. He tells of a sailor, long thought lost at sea, returning to his wife, who, with her father, runs a broken-down bar in a seaport. She is still an attractive woman, and their neighbour very much wants to marry her, but though he is an honourable and kind man and she likes him well enough she cannot bring herself to believe that her husband is dead, and she has never felt drawn to any other man. She would steal or even kill for her husband, she says; since no other man has ever appealed to her she has no difficulty in living virtuously. Her father calls her a fool, but she pays no attention.

When the husband returns he makes himself known to the neighbour and swears him to silence. Then he begs a night's shelter from his own wife and her father. They do not recognise him. He tells them that he is a friend and fellow-sailor of her husband's. They had been shipwrecked, and her husband had refused to sleep with the Queen of America, who desired him, because he wanted to remain faithful to his wife. What an idiot, says the father. The speaker, on the other hand, had no such scruples, satisfied the Queen, and departed loaded with gifts. He is now rich. The husband, though alive, is in hiding and in debt. As the guest goes to bed, the wife looks at him. For a moment he has a look of her husband. But this glimpse of the truth is withdrawn from her too swiftly to avert what is to follow. When the guest is asleep the wife comes to him and kills him by hammering his head in. His money will save the man she loves.

There are those who see in this opera nothing but a rather repulsive exercise in *grand guignol*, a recreation in terms of the France of the 1920s of the Italian *verismo* of the pre-1914 period. Supporters of the work see in it one of Cocteau's exercises in demonstrating the power of blind destiny. I incline to the second view. The piece has humanity. Only the father is a completely unsympathetic character. The others are strongly characterised, even though they be human instruments of fate. There is a feeling of tragic inevitability. The music is full of seaport sounds and the lilt of sailors' songs, waltzes and *javas*. It conjures up with skill the seamy but fascinating atmosphere of ports and docks.

So, in a healthy, breezy, English way, does Walton's Overture *Portsmouth Point*, written in 1925 and first heard at the Zürich Festival of the International Society for Contemporary Music in June the following year. This evokes Rowlandson's world of jolly if disreputable Jack Tars, doxies and tavern-keepers. It is something of a *genre* exercise, but its sound is plainly that of the 1920s—vigorous, rhythmic, raucous, tuneful. Definitely Portsmouth, not Toulon, still less Villefranche.

7

Africa and America

Negro Art   Jazz
The Latin American Influence

New York! ville des amoureux et des contre-jour.
—Jean Cocteau, *Les Mariés de la Tour Eiffel*
Aoua! Aoua! Méfiez-vous des blancs habitans du rivage.
—Evariste Parny, *Chansons madécasses*

Various strands contributed to the interest among creative musicians of the 1920s in the exotic as represented by Africa and America. There was first the attention paid by the Cubists and their predecessors to African plastic art, and the implied curiosity about the cultures from which this art sprang. In such hands as those of the French writer Blaise Cendrars and the English poet Nancy Cunard this extended to an interest in African literature, which resulted in the publication of 'negro anthologies'. There was also great excitement about jazz and ragtime (the two terms being often confused). These were variously seen as expressions of the negro soul; as sources which could be mined for useful rhythmic and harmonic devices; as a possible *lingua franca* for 'serious' composers; and as reflections of that exciting, enormous, glamorous country, America. The knowledge of jazz came partly from the infiltration of American musicians into Europe, partly from the perusal and frequent misunderstanding of printed music, partly from visits to America by musicians such as Milhaud.

A separate strand was the exploitation of South American musical styles and mannerisms, though in the works of certain composers this overlapped with the influence of jazz. Instances are such works as Milhaud's *L'Homme et son désir* and Lambert's *The Rio Grande,* and because of this overlapping the South American influence, such as it was, will be considered in the same bracket as the Afro-American one. It was, however, a logical continuation of the process by which composers of an earlier generation, notably Russians and Frenchmen, had drawn on the music of Spain as a source. Indeed it has often been said, and with some justice, that the best 'Spanish' music has been written by Frenchmen: witness Debussy's *Ibéria*, a work impossible to match among the music of the post-Pedrell Spanish musical renaissance.

I have mentioned the element of misunderstanding in the use musicians made of the sources on which they drew. This misunderstanding was sometimes technical in nature (whatever their merits, Stravinsky's *Ragtime* and his *Piano Rag-Music* are not jazz or ragtime in the sense that those terms are normally understood) and sometimes a misunderstanding of America itself. Sometimes the European artists *chose* to misunderstand. For instance, America provided Brecht with a convenient mythology on which to build, a capitalist never-never land he could use as a setting for his morality plays, and a source of evocative backgrounds, ideas and even place-names. This will become apparent in the discussion of *Mahagonny* (pp. 99–111). But none of these misunderstandings, total or partial, accidental or deliberate, matters much, and they certainly do not affect the status of the results as art. They must stand or fall on their own merits.

In Europe in the 1920s there were occasional attempts, not, in general, successful, at the creation of 'authentic' Americana. For instance, Rolf de Maré having decided that he wanted an authentic American ballet for his Company, Milhaud introduced him to a young American musician he had met at the house of the Princesse Edmond de Polignac, herself, it will be recalled, an American by birth. This was Cole Porter, who composed for de Maré a ballet about a young Swede and his experiences in New York. This was called *Within the Quota* and first presented in the same programme as Milhaud's *La Création du monde*. Porter did not (probably could not) make his own orchestrations, and this work was undertaken by Charles Koechlin, composer of the *Bandar-Log* symphonic poem which forms the bulk of the music for the Royal Ballet's *Shadowplay*. Gerald Murphy, who had been responsible for the book of *Within the Quota*, also made the designs. The work enjoyed some success and the Swedish Ballet took it to America with them in November 1923. The score was rediscovered in 1970, and proved pretty bad, with its pallid echoes of jazz, Milhaud and Stravinsky.

Before considering the composers on whom jazz, for a time at least, made a profound impact, it is convenient to deal with those established figures who flirted with jazz and those younger men who also played with it a little before coming to the conclusion that it was not, in any fundamental sense, for them.

Gabriel Pierné was a pillar of the French musical establishment, though he is largely and regrettably forgotten today, even his charming so-called *Entry of the Little Fauns* (from the ballet *Cydalise et le chèvre-pied*), once so popular, being hardly ever heard. Pierné was a highly accomplished composer, who followed the French tradition of providing agreeable, professional, deft entertainment music, not by any means to be despised. Some of his music can stand beside some of Fauré's, and it is a great pity that such minor masterpieces as the *Concertstück* for harp and orchestra are so little known. Pierné was also an excellent conductor, and directed the first performances of such very different works as *L'Oiseau de feu* and Milhaud's *Second Symphonic Suite, Protée*. From 1910 till 1934 he was chief conductor of the Concerts Colonne in Paris, and in 1931 he wrote, as a present for his Orchestra, the *Divertissements sur un thème pastoral, Op. 49*, which he dedicated to 'my dear friends and collaborators'. Appropriately, the Colonne Orchestra gave the work its first performance on 7 February, 1932. It is a pleasant and skilful piece of some fifteen minutes' duration, designed to show off in turn the various sections of the orchestra. Its longest section is called *Cortège-Blues*, a processional movement with jazzy syncopations and a feeling of mild melancholy. The title is 'amusing', but the section sits well in the context of the whole work, which includes such other *genre* pieces as a Viennese waltz.

A rather different and highly comic case is that of Eduard Künneke's *Tänzerische Suite*, written for performance at the 1928 Berlin Radio Exhibition and recorded under its composer's baton in Nazi days (together with two other Künneke works, of revolting sentimentality, called the *Lönslieder-Suite* and the *Biedermeier-Suite*). Künneke was a pupil of Max Bruch and primarily an operetta composer. His most famous piece was *Der Vetter aus Dingsda* ('The Cousin from Nowhere'), which included the number known in English as *I'm only a strolling vagabond*. 'The Poet of the Kurfürstendamm', as Künneke was known to his admirers, also modishly included in this operetta a *Batavia Foxtrot*. However his major exercise in 'jazz' was the aforementioned *Dance Suite*, written after a visit to America in 1925–6 and subtitled *Concerto Grosso in Five Movements for a Jazzband and a Symphony Orchestra*. The movements are *Overture* (*Tempo des foxtrot*), *Blues* (*Andante*), *Intermezzo*, *Valse mélancolique* (*Tempo di valse boston*) and a final *foxtrot*. This ludicrous work is not without a certain dotty charm, but it nowhere approaches the condition of jazz: indeed the composer of whom it most reminds one is the late Eric Coates, except that the latter was more inventive.

A trifle by a younger composer was the *Rapsodie nègre* of Poulenc, scored for piano, string quartet, flute, clarinet and baritone solo. This was related less to jazz than to the cult of Africana among the Cubists and writers such as Blaise Cendrars —except that Poulenc was quite unable to take the cult seriously. The words of the vocal section are gibberish attributed to a wholly imaginary black poet called Makoko Kangourou, and the whole thing is a joke. There are five sections: *Prélude, Ronde, Honoloulou* (vocal interlude), *Pastorale* and *Final*. The work was first given most successfully at one of Jane Bathori's concerts at the Théâtre du Vieux-Colombier (11 December, 1917). Ravel thought that it showed promise, but it did not point in any particular direction for Poulenc's future development (there are traces of jazz in *Les Biches*, as we have seen, but none of joke-Africana).

Ravel, a much older man, took a much deeper interest in jazz. This shows in at least four works, while a fifth is related to the fascination with things African. This is the *Chansons madécasses* (Madagascan Songs), to words by the creole poet Evariste Parny (1754–1801). Ravel wrote the songs in 1925–26 to a Coolidge commission. His music reflects the sensuality and, in the case of the second song, *Aoua!*, the violence of the words. This central section of the work is a warning against the duplicity of the whites of the coast. The work is a kind of quartet for voice, flute, 'cello and piano, dark in tone, percussive at times, and hard to perform successfully.

Ravel's *Violin Sonata*, written during 1923–7, and first played on 30 May, 1927 in Paris by Georges Enesco and the composer, has a *Blues* as its second movement. But this is one of Ravel's very few works which are not completely successful. His use of jazz is seen to much better effect in the opera *L'Enfant et les sortilèges*. Though first performed in 1925, this work was eight years in the making. Colette, the authoress of the libretto, submitted her text to Jacques Rouché, Director of the Paris Opéra, during the 1914–18 War. At that stage it was called *Ballet pour ma fille*. In 1917 Ravel agreed to collaborate on the work, but it took him some time to get started. By 1921 some of the music had been written down, and he declined an invitation to write extensive incidental music for James Elroy Flecker's *Hassan* on the grounds that he was too busy with the opera. One wonders however whether he would really have wished to write music for *Hassan* at this stage of his career: it was the sort of commission he could probably have undertaken with success at the time he was writing *Shéhérazade*, but by the 1920s the cult of the Mysterious East was beginning to seem very old hat in France, even if the English, behind-hand as usual, could still discern some charm in it. Or maybe he simply realised that *Hassan* is really a pretty dreadful play. His literary standards were high.

In 1924 Ravel began to concentrate on *L'Enfant et les sortilèges* to the exclusion of other things, and it received its first performance on 21 March the following year at Monte Carlo under Victor de Sabata. Ravel scored it for triple wood-wind, including an E flat clarinet, four horns, three trumpets, three trombones, tuba, fifteen percussion instruments, including piano and celesta, harp and strings. But this large orchestra is used with chamber-music delicacy, rather than with the opulence (also delicate) of the earlier *Daphnis and Chloe*.

The opera is the story of a naughty child who is prone to damage furniture, carve his name on trees, ill-treat animals and be rude to his mother. Through showing pity he achieves reconciliation with them all. It is appallingly difficult to stage. Archness is the ever-present danger. Like Janáček's *The Cunning Little Vixen*, Ravel's work can be an embarrassing experience to watch, rather than hear. Anthropomorphised animals, animated teapots and grandfather clocks, and a small boy who must be sung and acted by an adult female are not constituents that make for a staging free of embarrassment. The archness has nothing to do with the music. On the gramophone or on the air both works succeed perfectly. Perhaps, as has been suggested, the best answer might lie in making cartoon films of these operas, provided directors and designers of sufficient taste could be found.

A striking feature of *L'Enfant et les sortilèges* is the composer's habit of retreating behind musical 'masks', a device he was enabled, nay encouraged, to adopt by the nature of the action, and one which suited Ravel's withdrawn personality to perfection. One of these masks is a jazz mask. This is the duet for china cup and Wedgwood teapot that occurs after the memorable spoken interchange:

'How's your mug?'
'Rotten.'
'Better had. Come on . . .'

And they go into a foxtrot, sometimes played on its own and called *Le Five O'Clock*, into which Ravel introduces a certain amount of *chinoiserie* in allusion to the cup's country of origin. Writing about the work, Jeremy Noble said:

> Written a decade and a Great War later (than *L'Heure espagnole*), it cost Ravel far more effort to compose. The dandy's flawless elegance was no longer possible; the deliberately heartless mask had been fractured. Here, in fact, it is not a question of one mask but of many; Ravel takes every opportunity for parody, even persuading Colette to give him an extra one by turning her Auvergne cup and teapot into China and Wedgwood for an improbable foxtrot duet. But when all the chances for evasion have been taken (with the utmost skill, though not without damaging the work's musical consistency) the libretto compels him to show his own face at last in the amazingly original chorus leading up to the reborn child's final cry of 'Maman!' . . . Ravel himself snatches the moment of truth away as if embarrassed.*

Noble is concerned here with the chorus in which the animals and creatures of the garden join the frightened child

* *New Statesman and Nation*, 26 March, 1965.

in calling for his mother to come and help him. Their cries are heard over a pizzicato string accompaniment; then the 'Mother' theme is heard and the chorus embarks on the closing section with the words '*Il est bon, l'Enfant, il est sage*'. Towards the end, to almost unbearably moving effect, the meandering high woodwind heard at the beginning of the whole work returns over the choral line. The child utters the word 'Maman!' and, as the figure of his mother begins to appear, the opera ends abruptly. The work reveals Ravel's nature as clearly as Poulenc's *Aubade* does his.

Ravel's last important works were his twin *Piano Concertos*, one of them for the left hand alone and written for the Austrian pianist Paul Wittgenstein (brother of the philosopher) who had lost his right arm during the 1914–18 War. It was for him that Britten wrote his *Diversions*. One of the major disappointments of my early life was hearing Wittgenstein playing the Ravel at the Royal Albert Hall in London: by that stage he could no longer even manage the notes. The other *Concerto*, also composed in 1930–1, was written for two hands in the conventional manner. Both works show jazz influence, though there are other influences present as well: that of Spanish music in both and those of Mozart, Saint-Saëns and perhaps Fauré in the two-handed *Concerto*. Wittgenstein gave the first performance of one in Vienna on 27 November, 1931, Marguerite Long that of the other under the baton of the composer at the Salle Pleyel in Paris on 14 January, 1932.

The dark and stately Spanish sarabande which opens and closes the *Left Hand Concerto* has no feeling of jazz, but during the body of this one-movement work (the *Allegro*) the bassoon has a long, improvisatory but carefully notated passage in which it imitates the sound and phrasing of a jazz tenor saxophone; the episode builds up with something of the frightening relentlessness of the *Bolero*. In the *Piano Concerto in G* it is the outer, divertissement-like movements (the opening *Allegramente* and the final *Presto*) which reflect jazz; the central *Adagio assai* is classical in feeling and is one of its composer's finest inspirations. Much of the writing for piano, brass and percussion in the outer movements is jazzy, but comparisons with Gershwin are wide of the mark. Whatever the quality of his songs and musicals, Gershwin as serious composer had none of Ravel's fastidiousness and little of his professionalism, and the Ravel *Concerto* has a polish and sense of style which make Gershwin's two principal works for piano and orchestra, the *Concerto* and the *Rhapsody in Blue*, sound shoddy and shop-soiled.

In all the instances mentioned so far there was an element of flirtation between the composer and the jazz idiom. In the instances that remain the penetration was more profound. Aaron Copland, in his *Music for the Theater* (1925) and his *Piano Concerto* (1926), got to grips with the problem rather more deeply, but neither of these is among his best works and he did not truly find form until the 1930s, with works such as *Billy the Kid* and *El salón Mexico*, popular pieces which show him at his best. His attempts to don the mantle of the Great American Composer and write highly 'serious' and frequently serial music never quite seem to succeed, though Copland's is such an amiable personality that one hesitates to criticise. Speaking personally, I would give all his 'abstract' music—apart from the *Clarinet Concerto*, written for Benny Goodman and very jazzy—for the beautiful ballet *Appalachian Spring*. Bohuslav Martinů, a pupil of Roussel in Paris in the 1920s, ventured into the jazz area with his suite *La Revue de cuisine* and other small pieces, but his mature style shows little trace of these early exercises. Vladimir Dukelsky, a Diaghilev protégé who later changed his name to Vernon Duke, made a belated foray into jazz terrain with his ballet *Le Bal des blanchisseuses* (book by Boris Kochno, choreography by Roland Petit, sets by Stanislas Lepri), which the Ballets des Champs-Elysées gave in 1946. But though it was a charming ballet the music did not amount to much.

The four composers of the 1920s on whose music jazz made the most profound impact were Darius Milhaud, Kurt Weill, Ernst Křenek and Constant Lambert. I have dealt with Lambert at length elsewhere, and his *Piano Sonata*, *Piano Concerto* and *The Rio Grande* constitute a highly intelligent and largely successful attempt to apply lessons learned from jazz to the creation of serious compositions. I propose leaving consideration of Křenek and Weill till later, since many other important elements entered into their 'jazz-inspired' works, while Weill, at least, is a very large subject, his best compositions of high importance in the musical output of the twentieth century. The rest of this chapter, then, will be almost entirely concerned with Milhaud.

Milhaud's principal work in jazz idiom is the ballet *La Création du monde*, first performed by the Swedish Ballet at the Champs-Elysées Theatre on 25 October, 1923, with choreography by Borlin and sets and costumes by Léger. The idea for the ballet came from the poet Blaise Cendrars' *Negro Anthology*, and specifically from the section called *Légendes cosmogoniques*, black stories of the creation of the world. During the action the three gods of creation, Nzamé, Mébère and N'Kwa appear, together with the *Grandes Fétiches*. At the end, as the newly created moon and stars light up, the man, Sékoumé, and the woman, Mbongwé, kiss for the first time.

Milhaud conceived the work for an orchestra of soloists, consisting of seventeen players plus a pianist, on the lines of the negro bands he had heard in Harlem. The music contains episodes of the greatest rhythmic excitement, as well as passages of deep tenderness. After a slow introduction, containing a series of hints of the animation that is to come, the three gods appear to a jazz fugato. After a very brief blues-like passage, and a reprise of the material of the introduction, the music again grows very fast, and Stravinskian in character, though this in no way jars with the overall style of the piece. The term 'Stravinskian' in this case is used to indicate a certain amount of derivation from the works of Stravinsky's 'Swiss' period, a time when the Russian himself was coming under jazz influence to some extent. Fast and slow passages alternate until an extremely loud final outburst, ushering in the gentle, tender final pages. The work is arguably a masterpiece, without the 'dating' features which inevitably colour, though they do not prevent, one's enjoyment of *Le Boeuf sur le Toit*. Unhappily, apart from a short piece, the shimmy *Caramel mou*, Milhaud did not pursue the path indicated by *La Création*, and in his later works the jazz influence disappears almost entirely.

The Latin American element, however, constantly recurred. Its first important appearance in Milhaud's work occurred in the ballet *L'Homme et son désir*, written in Brazil during 1916–17, and first performed by the Swedish Ballet (6 June, 1921, Champs-Elysées Theatre), with choreography by Borlin and sets designed, somewhat improbably, by Audrey Parr, the wife of the secretary of the British Legation at Rio de Janeiro during Milhaud's stay there. The work sprang from an idea by Paul Claudel, whose secretary Milhaud had been while in Brazil. It was described as a *poème plastique*. Milhaud scored his music for a vocal quartet, singing wordlessly, a string quintet, a wind quintet, trumpet, harp and a great deal of percussion. The ballet is an evocation of the sounds of the Amazonian jungle, and is comparable with certain works of the native Brazilian Villa-Lobos, such as his *Nonetto*, modestly entitled 'an impression of the whole of Brazil'. Milhaud's work reveals a very secure hand for so young a man.

So does *Protée*. This was incidental music for another work of Claudel's, the satyr-play *Proteus*, not presented with Milhaud's music until a production at Groningen in 1929. Milhaud drew a suite from it, the *Symphonic Suite No. 2*, which received a hostile reaction when Pierné conducted it at a Paris concert in October 1920. The two movements which most upset the audience were a dissonant fugue representing Proteus' seals at play and an equally abrasive finale. The *Pastorale* is based on a South American rhythm, while the beautiful *Nocturne* is one of Milhaud's loveliest inspirations, its high singing violin line typifying what the composer called his 'Mediterranean lyricism'.

There was no reason why Latin American features should intrude into a play set on a Greek island: Milhaud simply thought that it was a good idea. Likewise, in *Salade*, the sung ballet which Milhaud wrote for de Beaumont (first performance on 17 May, 1924, with scenario and text by Albert Flament, sets by Braque, and choreography by Massine; conductor—Roger Desormière), there is a point at which the corps, for no apparent reason (since the action is based on the *commedia dell'arte*), put on South American hats and go into a tango. This was the number which Milhaud called *Souvenir de Rio* when he rearranged much of the score for piano and orchestra and called it *Le Carnaval d'Aix*. The work begins appropriately enough with the traditional Italian tune also used by Liszt in his *Canzonetta del Salvator Rosa*. There is also much use of Latin Americana, tangos and beguines, in Milhaud's three miniature operas, spoofs of mythological subjects, the *opéras-minutes* *L'Enlèvement d'Europe*, *L'Abandon d'Ariane* and *La Délivrance de Thésée*. Each of these has a libretto of some wit by Henri Hoppenot and each lasts about eight minutes. Milhaud has thus written some of the biggest and some of the smallest operas in musical history. His only obvious competitor at miniature length is Samuel Barber, whose *A Hand of Bridge* (written for Spoleto to a libretto by Gian-Carlo Menotti), witty and touching, earthy and elegant, is of roughly the same duration as Milhaud's little pieces (though with more of a claim to immortality: in its tiny span it is perfect). The first of the *opéra-minutes*, *L'Enlèvement d'Europe*, was first given at the 1927 contemporary music festival at Baden-Baden (17 July), in distinguished company: Hindemith's *Hin und Zurück*, Ernst Toch's *Die Prinzessin auf der Erbse* ('The Princess and the Pea') and *Das kleine Mahagonny* of Kurt Weill.

Milhaud's most famous and popular exercise in Latin American style is undoubtedly the *Brasileira* which forms the finale of his three-movement suite for two pianos, *Scaramouche*, which the composer put together in 1937 for the duo-pianists Ida Jankelevitch and Marcelle Meyer. The two outer movements (*Vif* and the *Brasileira*) came from incidental music for Molière's play *Le Médecin volant* in an adaptation by Charles Vildrac. This had been presented by the Théâtre Scaramouche, a company specialising in producing plays for audiences of children. The gaiety and verve of the *Brasileira* has made it better known than any other work of Milhaud's.

If only to show that Milhaud did not command a total monopoly in this area one should mention Mexican and Brazilian composers themselves, as well as the century's most famous exercise in Spanish or Latin American style, the *Bolero* of Ravel, written as a ballet for Ida Rubinstein and first given as such in 1928 with choreography by Nijinska and sets by Benois. It has never worked as a ballet, mainly, once again, because it is hard to match the cumulative excitement of the music in terms of stage movement. It has been highly praised, over-performed, reviled, described as sinister and hysterical. It is certainly a virtuoso exercise in orchestration and in sustained melody (though, of course, it has only one).

Finally, to return momentarily to the cult of things negro, an event of the highest importance in theatrical terms occurred in Paris in 1925. When Rolf de Maré wound up his ballet company he turned to other enterprises, and that year he presented Paris with the *Revue nègre*, starring Josephine Baker, making her first appearance in the city she was to delight and excite for so long. At long last, through her and through the Blackbirds, the cult of negro art, which began among the Fauve and Cubist painters, and which reached an elite through the medium of the ballet, penetrated to the general public.

8

Speech and Song in the Ballet

Prima la Musica e poi le Parole.
—Abbé Casti

An interesting development in ballet in the 1920s was the fondness of certain composers for using singers as well as the orchestra in their scores. It is necessary however to distinguish between the choral ballet on the one hand and the *mélodrame* on the other (I leave the word *mélodrame* untranslated, since the English associations of the word 'melodrama' are all wrong in this case).

The *mélodrame* was a characteristically French form with a long history. Its roots lay in French literary and musical tradition. It was an entertainment using music, both played and sung, dance and speech. The speech was frequently superimposed on the music, and this is an essential feature of the form. As much as any factor, it owed its revival in the twentieth century to the dancer Ida Rubinstein, who originally appeared in the West as a member of the Diaghilev Ballet. At this time of her life Rubinstein was rich, and though she ran through her personal fortune in the end (it will soon be clear why) she was able in the post-1918 years to find rich backers who admired her exotic beauty. She was not in fact a very good dancer: though she mimed and moved well, she lacked technique. This was one reason why she did not remain for long with Diaghilev. There was a limited number of roles for which she was suited, because of the technical limitations I have mentioned, and she could not in any case expect to hog the limelight when Diaghilev could call on the services of such superb dancers as Karsavina and Pavlova.

Another reason for leaving Diaghilev was that Rubinstein was anxious to appear continually in works of which she was the indisputable star. This led to her creating her own company. In 1911 she offered herself to the public in the first of her 'creations', *Le Martyre de Saint-Sébastien*. The roster of collaborators could hardly have been more distinguished: Debussy for the music, Gabriele d'Annunzio for the words, Bakst for the sets, Fokine for the dances, Inghelbrecht to conduct. But the work was not a triumph, though Rubinstein revived it as late as 1931 during her Covent Garden season that year. Debussy's contribution was very extensive but was completed in haste, with help from André Caplet. This single work had a profound effect on Caplet's own style of composition: indeed it dominated all the rest of his works.

Various laudable attempts have been made to keep *Le Martyre* alive. Inghelbrecht himself used regularly to present it in oratorio form in Paris, as if it were the French *Parsifal*, which, in a sense, it is. It is fortunate too that he also recorded the work, for his performance has an authenticity lacking in other recordings. De Sabata once conducted a staged performance at La Scala, which one imagines would have been electrifying. There have been various recordings, with all of the spoken text, some of it, or none of it. Charles Munch himself spoke some of the text in his own American recording. A suite of 'symphonic fragments' has been drawn from the work. It has not been allowed to die. Nor must it, since it contains extraordinary and moving music. Yet it is the supreme illustration of what might be called the Rubinstein tragedy.

Again and again she assembled similar teams to create works for her personal glorification. There were d'Annunzio, Ildebrando Pizzetti and Bakst for the Cypriot extravaganza *La Pisanella* (1913), which ends with the heroine being smothered to death with roses; Paul Valéry, Honegger, Massine and Benois for *Amphion* (1931); Valéry, Honegger, Fokine and Jakovlev for *Semiramis* (1934); Jacques Ibert, Fokine and Dmitri Bouchenne for *Diane de Poitiers* (1934); Paul Claudel and Honegger for *Jeanne d'Arc au bûcher*. For *Perséphone* (Paris Opéra, 30 April, 1934), Rubinstein commissioned music from Stravinsky on a text by André Gide, choreography from Kurt Jooss, designs from André Barsacq. The stage properties were by Cartier, which just about sums the whole thing up. This is far from being a complete list.

It will not have escaped the reader's attention that each of these enterprises centres around a single character, usually but not invariably female (Rubinstein liked the occasional *travesti* role). Naturally, there had to be other ballets for the company to dance, in which Rubinstein did not appear, but the most lavish expenditure of money and talent went on works which were to star the leading figure of the company: herself. She was never a great dancer; she did not improve with age; and there have been many who spoke French words better than she. The result was a number of highly expensive enterprises doomed from the start to failure or at least a success that could be only partial. In consequence a series of rescue operations has had to be performed in order to quarry from these works the long stretches of fine music which almost every one of them contains.

I do not wish to appear too sour about Ida Rubinstein. After all, without her, much beautiful music would not have been written. But it was truly a tragedy that she felt unable to abstain from making herself the central figure on every occasion. Patronesses of the ballet are not always like this. The admirable Miss Lucia Chase, for instance, poured large sums and much effort into the creation and administration of American National Ballet Theater, and asked little more than the satisfaction of knowing what she had created and the chance to appear occasionally in small parts. She did not seek to be the centre of attention. Luckily, too, she was a very workmanlike dancer. It was only when she ventured into the classical repertoire that one felt a vague unease. Her mime, in particular, left something to be desired. There was, for instance, a point in Act 1 of her company's rather Disneyland *Lac des Cygnes* where Miss Chase, as Princess Mother, appeared to be making strenuous suggestions to her son that it was really time that he went and shot himself a bride. Still, such things were a small price to pay for the pleasure she had given to so many with her Company.

The record companies have played a noble part in mounting rescue operations to save the music of the Rubinstein repertoire. But alas, so far as they are concerned, Ida Rubinstein's mantle, if such it can be called, has fallen, heavily, on the shoulders of Vera Zorina, or rather, to give her her real name, Eva Birgitta Hartwig, a Berlin-born Norwegian and one-time wife (like so many) of Balanchine, who after dancing with the de Basil Company for a couple of years moved into films. She has recorded *Le Martyre*, *Perséphone* and *Jeanne d'Arc* (twice), as well as the beautiful little Debussy-Louÿs *Chansons de Bilitis* in the 'realisation' by Pierre Boulez. Each of these is a fine work; it is all the more maddening that in these recordings musical performances of high quality have had to contend with Miss Zorina's French, which could be described, depending on one's charitability, as highly unidiomatic or plain bad.

There was an attempt to revive *Jeanne d'Arc* at the now defunct Stoll Theatre in London in 1954, with Ingrid Bergman in the title role and a production by her then husband, the film director Roberto Rossellini. The work is a complex one in some ways, and the musical standards in the performance were not high; moreover the male corps de ballet minced even more than was usual at the time, a period in the history of British ballet which might, to paraphrase Ivor Novello, have been described as *The Mincing Years*. The general effect was unsatisfactory.

Perséphone is an even sadder case. Stravinsky wrote it for reciter (Rubinstein), tenor, mixed chorus and orchestra. Paul Valéry admired it greatly and wrote to Stravinsky that '*le divin détachement de votre oeuvre m'a touché*'. But it had been an unhappy collaboration. Stravinsky referred to Gide's Parnassian poetry as *vers de caramel*, while Gide was perturbed by the Russian's disregard for the usual rules of French prosody. Yet the music is often superb. Stravinsky's sense of ritual, already noticed, is much in evidence. Robert Craft has spoken of the 'Russian Easter' feeling of the final chorus, and the various Choruses of the Shades in the second part, *Perséphone aux Enfers*, capture to an extraordinary and moving degree the feeling of souls not in torment but in limbo, endlessly repeating the same actions:

> *Ici rien ne s'achève*
> *Ici chacun poursuit*
> *Chacun poursuit sans trève*
> *Ce qui s'écoule et fuit . . .*
> *Les ombres ne sont pas malheureuses.*
> *Sans haine et sans amour, sans peine et sans envie*
> *Elles n'ont pas d'autre destin*

Que de recommencer sans fin
Le geste inachevé de la vie.

Gide's words are not without distinction, it will be observed;
and the way Stravinsky sets the last lines, with a sensation of
movement continually turning back on itself, is masterly.
Frederick Ashton gamely attempted a revival of the work in
December, 1961. Svetlana Beriosova, in the Rubinstein part,
moved around the stage with a microphone concealed about
her person and, so far as could be divined above the general
mêlée, was speaking beautiful French. She also, of course,
looked lovely. But Nico Ghika's sets and costumes were of the
kind that are usually described as a riot of colour, and Ashton
was well below his best: notably when Alexander Grant as
Mercury was encouraged to play for laughs with no musical
or literary justification whatsoever. Persephone was indeed a
fille mal gardée but she was not *La Fille mal gardée*. Mention has
already been made of Honegger's sensible action in extracting
an orchestral work from *Amphion* (p. 33), and Ibert did
as much for his *Diane de Poitiers*.

The choral or sung ballet was, and remains, a proposition
more theatrically viable than the *mélodrame*. It has a far better
chance of 'coming off'. The fact that the music is sung as well
as played does nothing to hold up the action, and there is a
long folk tradition of dancing to sung music. The form was not
an invention of the 1920s: its roots in art music go back at
least to Monteverdi, whose *Ballo dell' ingrate* remains one of
the most beautiful of choral ballets. In the nineteenth and early
twentieth centuries composers of ballet sometimes made use
of an off-stage chorus. There is the *Waltz of the Snowflakes* in
Casse-noisette; the important choral element in *Daphnis and
Chloe*; and Florent Schmitt introduced a chorus into his
elaborate work, *La Tragédie de Salomé*. But the choral ballet to
end all choral ballets is surely *Les Noces* (pp. 44–6).

Pulcinella too, which is vocal, though not choral, has already
been considered, as has *Les Biches*. Two composers less well
known than Stravinsky and Poulenc, Vittorio Rieti and Nicolas
Nabokov, used singers in their ballets *Barabau* and *Ode*, both
written for Diaghilev. *Barabau* (London Coliseum, 11 December,
1925) was a choral ballet with choreography by Balanchine

and sets by Maurice Utrillo. It was a knockabout farce, set in Italy, in which a rich, sly peasant feigned death to trick soldiers intent on pillage. The Sadler's Wells Ballet revived it in 1936 with designs by Burra. The style of the music is heavily influenced by Stravinsky, especially in the *Sergeant's Dance*, but it has a certain vivacity.

Ode has not survived save in the printed score and through the medium of Tchelitchew's extraordinary designs. Diaghilev had wanted a ballet which would evoke the court of the eighteenth-century Empress Elizabeth of Russia, who loved art and disliked Germans. Her favourite poet was Mikhail V. Lomonosov, author of a poem called the 'Ode to the Grandeur of Nature and to the Aurora Borealis'. But Tchelitchew made of the ballet something mystical and astonishing (Théâtre Sarah Bernhardt, 6 June, 1928). Massine was responsible for the choreography. In W. A. Propert's description the ballet sounds fascinating. In a scene called 'Flowers and Mankind'

> intricate and lovely figures of flowers and men were projected on to the deep blue background, while in front of it nature and the 'Light Speck' (Lifar) played ball with an immense crystal sphere that glittered with all the colours of the prism.*

Weill's 'Ballet with Song' *The Seven Deadly Sins of the Petit-Bourgeois* is almost as fine as *Les Noces*, musically though not balletically, but through style and subject-matter it belongs in a later chapter. Later essays in choral ballet included works by Lord Berners, Gian-Carlo Menotti and another piece by Rieti.

A Wedding Bouquet (1937) by Berners was a slight but amusing half-echo of *Les Noces*, with sets and costumes as well as music by Berners and choreography by Ashton. It was an entertaining evocation of a French provincial wedding, its words, by Gertrude Stein, making about as much sense as hers usually do but conveying none the less at times a sharp ironic comment on the action.

These words are scored to be sung by a chorus, though during the 1939–45 War a single speaker (Constant Lambert) took over most successfully. After the War the ballet was

* *The Russian Ballet 1921–1929*, 1932.

revived at Covent Garden with a chorus, but it lapsed from the repertory in 1951. When it was brought back in November 1964, Robert Helpmann, once the Bridegroom, took the words over and attempted to emulate Lambert, without success. He overacted and overpointed the words (a similar mistake has been made by many reciters of Walton's *Façade*, Hermione Gingold and Cleo Laine being particularly bad offenders in this respect). Berners' score is admirable in the theatre but not well suited to concert performance.

The last two ballets that deserve mention were both New York City Ballet productions (strictly the first was produced by that company's predecessor, Ballet Society). This was *The Triumph of Bacchus and Ariadne*, a ballet-cantata for soprano and bass soli, chorus and orchestra (1948) by Rieti, whose aim was to evoke the carnival entertainments of Florence in the days of Lorenzo de' Medici. The other was Gian-Carlo Menotti's work *The Unicorn, the Gorgon and the Manticore*, described as a *madrigal fable* for chorus, ten dancers and nine instruments. The madrigals are part songs, if the truth be told, but it is a pleasant piece, with Menotti's usual deftness, much underestimated, at least in Britain.

9

Germany

Immediately you are over the Rhine, the spirit of the place has changed.
—D. H. Lawrence

Almost all the musical activity so far described was concentrated in France. By no means all the music was written by Frenchmen, but Paris was a magnet for musicians as well as for writers and artists. In addition, the Diaghilev Ballet and its rivals were based in France, and there was always the hope of prestigious, though not necessarily rewarding, commissions. The idea of Paris as a magnet for musicians is bound to seem a little odd today, when standards in the French capital have declined so disastrously. It is to be hoped that the efforts of Rolf Liebermann and Pierre Boulez continue to effect an improvement.

Germany in the 1920s presented a picture as rich, or richer, from the musical point of view. In particular Berlin, which until the 1870s had been merely the Prussian capital, and which even under the imperialist regime of Wilhelm II had remained somewhat dowdy and provincial, grew enormously in size and blossomed artistically. It became an international capital as culturally interesting as Paris, though in a very different way.

It supported three opera houses. There was the Städtische Oper, which, in the late 1920s, was under the control of Bruno Walter as *Generalmusikdirektor*. The State Opera had two separate establishments: Oper unter den Linden, presided over by Erich Kleiber, with Leo Blech as his assistant, and the Oper am Platz der Republik, where the *Generalmusikdirektor* at the time was Otto Klemperer, assisted by Georg Szell, Alexander Zemlinsky and Fritz Zweig. This last house was normally known as the Kroll Oper.

Klemperer in particular did much at this stage of his career for contemporary opera. It is a pity, I think, that during his later years, when he at last achieved in Britain the reputation that was his due, he concentrated so much, either through personal choice or through the wishes of others, on the works of Beethoven, with occasional Mozart and Mahler performances. It would have been most interesting to hear him direct more modern works.

He went to work permanently in Berlin in 1927, having come from Wiesbaden, and, before that, Cologne. He introduced many modern works into the repertory of the Kroll Oper during his tenure of office, which finished in 1931, when the Kroll Oper, which had aroused much criticism and come under intense attack, closed (Klemperer moved for two years to the Oper unter den Linden). In 1928 he performed Stravinsky's *Oedipus Rex*, *Mavra* and *L'Histoire du soldat*, Hindemith's *Cardillac* and a triple bill of operas by Křenek; in 1929 he gave the premiere of Hindemith's *Neues vom Tage;* in 1930 he presented Hindemith's *Hin und Zurück*, Schönberg's *Die glückliche Hand* and Křenek's *Das Leben des Orest* (with designs by Giorgio de Chirico). In that same year Kleiber gave the the world premiere of Milhaud's *Christophe Colomb* at his opera house (5 May); this work, which was written on a vast scale and used film as well as other devices, enjoyed an enormous success at the time, but a revival in the early 1970s (relayed by the European Broadcasting Union) did not confirm these high opinions. Increasingly Milhaud is seen as a composer who worked best on a smaller scale.

Berlin's status as a musical capital of the highest importance was confirmed by the Berlin Festival of 1929, during which Toscanini conducted *Falstaff* with Mariano Stabile, *Il trovatore* with Lauri-Volpi and *Manon Lescaut* with Pertile, Pampanini and Salvatore Baccaloni; Richard Strauss directed *Der Rosenkavalier*, *Die Frau ohne Schatten* and *Die Aegyptische Helena;* Klemperer offered *Don Giovanni* and *Neues vom Tage*, as well as a concert at which Stravinsky played his own *Piano Concerto;* Leo Blech directed Busoni's *Doktor Faust* and a complete *Ring;* Fürtwangler conducted the Berlin Philharmonic Orchestra; and Kleiber contributed *Wozzeck*, Schreker's *Der singende Teufel* and a concert performance of *La clemenza di Tito*.

Such musical riches were seldom if ever equalled outside Germany. Of course, the Festival was an exceptional event, but all Germany was musically rich. Its history had led to this, since until the latter part of the nineteenth century the country had consisted of a number of small states, and even after the union under Prussia these had preserved a certain autonomy. Every town and city of significance had—and has— its own opera house, and there was naturally rivalry between them to outdo each other in excellence. It was for instance at the Württemburgisches Staatstheater that Strauss's *Ariadne auf Naxos* received its first performance in a production by Max Reinhardt. Hence, alongside the growing prestige and importance of Berlin, there was musical activity of a high order at such cities as Dresden, Leipzig, Munich, Hamburg and Stuttgart, to name only the leading musical centres.

This activity took many forms, and though it is new music which concerns us here it is worth noting the 'Verdi Revival' which occurred in Germany in the 1920s. Not that the Italians had ever neglected their greatest nineteenth-century composer, but they had seldom devoted to him the concentrated care in production which German musicians now gave him.

It is all the more extraordinary that this intense creativity took place against a background of economic collapse, political instability, ever-growing lawlessness and ever-darkening prospects for the future. The contrast with France could not have been more marked. I have spoken of the prevalent atmosphere of hedonism in much of the music written in France at this time. France was still, in a sense, the playground of Europe. It had, after all, won the War, though not without appalling losses and suffering. Gloom did not reign. The French temperament in general is not prone to depression and melancholia. And much of what was created was, as we have seen, designed in the first instance for the ears and eyes of a rich, pleasure-loving, cultivated segment of society.

Germany had lost the War. People were poor. Cynicism was understandably rife. Sensitive people feared for what was to become of their country. Germans are not conspicuous for cheerful optimism. These fears and this cynicism are abundantly reflected in the music of the period in Germany, above all in that of its most characteristic and most gifted composer, Kurt Weill.

In French music, and in the music of those whose aesthetic

approach was influenced by French thinking, there were certain paramount influences, such as Satie and Stravinsky. The position was less clear in Germany. Busoni exerted great prestige by example, and the posthumous production of his largest work, the opera *Doktor Faust*, added to this prestige. Mahler's influence was not much acknowledged, but one can hear it from time to time. Many musicians looked back to the classical composers of the eighteenth century, notably to Bach, but their neoclassicism, if such it can be called, was of a different kind from the style prevailing in France and it seems to me that Stravinsky as intermediary was not a significant factor. There was also a continuing influence exerted in certain quarters by Franz Schreker, a composer highly successful in his own day though largely forgotten now. His works merit revival. He used—and continued throughout the 1920s to use, with progressively less and less acclaim—a very rich and highly eclectic brand of late romanticism as vehicle for ideas not unrelated to those of the dramatist Wedekind. Křenek was a Schreker pupil, and it is also possible to see some connection between the operas of Schreker and some of the earlier works of Weill, notably *Royal Palace*. A much younger and very brilliant composer, the Austrian Jewish *Wunderkind* Erich Korngold, achieved much success with his opera *Die tote Stadt*, but his music was frankly backward-looking, combining elements of Strauss, Puccini and even Franz Léhar in a mixture that had much appeal for the public but was well away from the mainstreams of contemporary music. One of these, represented by the Second Viennese School, does not concern us here. The other centred round a trio of young composers, each very different from the other. These were Paul Hindemith, Ernst Křenek and Kurt Weill.

It is sad to have to say that none of this highly gifted trio completely fulfilled the expectations aroused by his early achievements. Alas for the hopes of youth: in later years Weill was to become a composer of musicals, Hindemith a Kappellmeister, Křenek (most melancholy fate of all) a serialist. The reasons for these lamentable developments will shortly appear.

Paul Hindemith (1895–1963) was almost as productive as Milhaufl or Villa-Lobos, and his music was as uneven as that

of either. Much of his output suffers from a prevalent greyness
and drabness, an impression reinforced in his later work, where
the apparently innovatory quality of his earlier music had
disappeared. Basically an academic, he reacted dutifully and
industriously to the prevailingly cynical and satirical atmosphere of the 1920s, which he mirrored with Teutonic
thoroughness. At this stage his music had the exuberance of
youth, though it could not be said to have had its charm. The
ruthlessness of his contrapuntal procedures gave him a
reputation as an atonalist, an epithet loosely used at this time
and one which Hindemith never deserved.

He was extremely active throughout the decade as composer,
organiser and performer (he was an outstanding violist and a
competent performer on many other instruments). In the
later years of the period he concerned himself very much with
the composition of music suitable for performance by amateurs
—works such as the *Lehrstück* of 1929, to a text by Brecht, in
which it was intended that the audience should participate. He
evolved the theory of *Gebrauchsmusik* (roughly translatable as
'utility music'), which enjoyed a certain vogue and which
spawned a certain progeny. But the progeny—which included,
years later, Copland's *The Second Hurricane* and Britten's *Let's
Make an Opera*—produced more truly 'useful' (because more
pleasurable) music than the Hindemith works which began
the movement.

There is something more than a little depressing about
Hindemith's antlike productivity in the 1920s. However it is
necessary to mention two works of his which are examples of
the so-called *Zeitoper*—opera which tried to mirror contemporary life as it was lived, and of which the most famous
and hilarious example was not by Hindemith but by Ernst
Křenek.

Both the Hindemith works were written on libretti by
Marcellus Schiffer, a writer of revue sketches. They could be
described as tabloid operas. In the first, the short piece called
Hin und Zurück ('There and Back'), action and music go into
complete reverse half way through. In the second, a full-
length opera called *Neues vom Tage* ('News of the Day'), first
given on 8 June, 1929, at the Kroll Oper, love duet is replaced
by hate duet, wedding ensemble by divorce ensemble, and so

forth. This kind of mechanical reversal is entirely typical of Hindemith's painstaking, literal, tidy mind. In more conformist times he would have written conformist works, and indeed, in time, his music assumed an obviously academic manner. He was the modern Reger.

Ernst Křenek (1900–) was a more complex figure. He first went through what was generally called a period of 'free atonality', during which he produced several operas: the 'scenic cantata' *Die Zwingburg* on words by Franz Werfel (Berlin, Staatsoper, 21 October 1924); *Der Sprung über den Schatten*, to his own libretto (Frankfort, 9 June, 1924); and *Orpheus und Eurydike* on words by the painter and poet Kokoschka (Cassel, 27 November, 1926). In the latter two he began to introduce jazz elements into his music. But it was during 1925–6 that he wrote the work which made him an international celebrity. This was the *Zeitoper, Jonny spielt auf* ('Johnny strikes up').

This was first given at Leipzig on 10 February, 1927. It was an enormous success. It was translated into eighteen languages and produced in about a hundred opera houses. It made Křenek's fortune and enabled him to retire from his post at the Wiesbaden Opera House and thereafter to write when, how and what he chose, with disastrous results.

The principal characters in *Jonny spielt auf* are Max, a composer, Anita, an opera singer, Daniello, a white virtuoso violinist, Yvonne, a chambermaid, and Jonny, who is a negro jazz band leader and also a virtuoso of the violin (this sets the tone for the whole opera; who has ever heard of a virtuoso jazz violinist, apart from Stéphane Grappelly?)

Max is a brooding intellectual with a habit of rushing off when under stress to commune with nature on his favourite glacier. Anita, whom he loves, falls victim to the oily charm of Daniello and becomes estranged from Max. Meanwhile Yvonne, who for all the opera's 'modernity' is the classic opera and operetta soubrette, has become entangled with Jonny. Jonny steals Daniello's violin (which seems to have semi-magic qualities, like the instrument in *L'Histoire du soldat*), and eventually poor Max is arrested and charged with this theft. In the end the disagreeable Daniello, during a tussle with Yvonne, falls under the Amsterdam train and is killed.

Max and Anita are reunited, and at the end Jonny is seen standing on a shining model of the earth, bestriding the North Pole, and playing his violin like anything.

It will be seen at once that the *Zeitoper* as exemplified by *Jonny spielt auf* is not at all about real life as experienced by most people. Then as now, few people moved in a world peopled by glamorous opera singers, violin virtuosi, jazz band leaders and composers. The opera was in fact a picture of the sort of world people read about in the gossip columns of the newspapers, a vicarious peek into the exciting world of the Jet Set. The opera created a *frisson* by having a black man as hero, and by presenting him as the symbol of a race that was taking the world over. There were riots when *Jonny* was presented in Munich, because of resentment against the black American soldiers serving in the Rhineland. When the opera was staged at Dresden, shortly after the Leipzig premiere, the young Paul Schöffler took the part of Jonny. He had become engaged to a young Englishwoman studying in Dresden, Mary Lubbock.' Her brother Mark mischievously sent the Lubbock family a photograph of his sister's fiancé in the character of Jonny, thereby causing considerable consternation till the truth was revealed.

Křenek's own libretto, then, was a silly one, but it was well calculated to create the effect he was seeking. And after all many opera libretti are silly. The staging at Leipzig was spectacular: the locomotive which put paid to Daniello appeared on stage in the best Drury Lane manner. But the music's extreme eclecticism reinforces one's impression of cynical opportunism in the whole enterprise. There is old-fashioned if rather chilly romanticism, trendy modern harshness, and a Teutonic version of jazz which is extremely funny and serves to demonstrate, if demonstration were needed, that jazz and the German soul are uncomfortable bedmates, except in the hands of a near-genius. It is a clever work but a meretricious one, and despite its huge success at the time it cannot be taken with a grain of seriousness any more. In this respect it contrasts very sharply with Weill's *Aufstieg und Fall der Stadt Mahagonny*, produced at Leipzig three years later, which contains just as many disparate ingredients as *Jonny* but contrives to weld them together into a satisfactory whole.

Mahagonny can still make a great impact on audiences. The superficial similarities between the two works fade away when the utter seriousness and tragic force of Weill's work become apparent. It is so important and so good that I propose discussing it at length on a later page.

Křenek's next considerable work was *Das Leben des Orest*, an opera in five acts on a libretto by the composer which was written in 1928–9 and first produced at Leipzig in the same year as *Mahagonny* (19 January, 1930). In this Křenek added romantic or 'neo-Schubertian' ingredients to the mix, which still included jazz of a kind. The work was revived in Germany after the 1939–45 War and enjoyed a certain success with the public. Křenek did not evolve a consistent style until he embraced serialism, thus, in effect, turning his back on the public. He could do this because *Jonny* had virtually enabled him to retire. His later career does not concern us here.

10

Kurt Weill

Ihr habt gelernt das Cocktail-abc,
ihr habt den Mond die ganze Nacht gesehn.
Geschlossen ist die Bar von Mandelay,
und es ist immer noch nichts geschehn.*

Kurt Weill (1900–50) was a far more considerable figure than Křenek, and, in my opinion, a far more important one than Hindemith also. Much of the music which he composed in the late 1920s and early 1930s is of major importance. He is also something of an enigma and something of a tragedy.

Weill's music falls naturally into 'three periods', but not by any means the traditional three periods which critics have detected in the music of Beethoven or Bartók. In the first period (roughly 1920–7) Weill was considered a modernist, even an 'atonalist' (which he never was: the application of the term to him stemmed, as with Hindemith, from incomprehension). During this period he wrote highbrow music which reached only minority audiences. Then, falling under the influence of Brecht, Weill popularised his style without cheapening it and wrote works which achieved a high degree of communication with the public. Finally, after some uncertainty, Weill became a composer of Broadway musicals, good of their kind but much inferior to his earlier achievements. The reasons for this final development will be discussed later.

Weill was born in Dessau, the son of a cantor. He studied under Humperdinck and Busoni, among others, and the latter had much influence on him. The strain of what one might loosely call neoclassicism in Weill came to him via Busoni rather than via Stravinsky. Strauss, Mahler and Schönberg

---

* 'You have drunk all the cocktails from A to Z;
You have seen the moon all night.
The bar of Mandalay is closed,
And nothing has happened yet.'

—Bert Brecht, *Mahagonny*

were influences on Weill as a young man, though it was
Schönberg the atonal romantic rather than Schönberg the
doctrinaire serialist who impressed Weill. The result is to be
heard in the *Symphony No. 1* of 1921, an impressive student work
which Weill never released for public performance. The
influence of Strauss did not last, but that of Mahler did: it is
still very much there in the music Weill was writing in 1933.

During the 1920–7 period Weill's music was brought out in
the normal way for a promising young German composer of
the period, in opera houses and at avant-garde festivals. It
made little impression on the non-specialist general public.
Among the music he wrote at this time was a 'pantomime' or
children's ballet, *Die Zaubernacht* (Berlin, 1923), and three
short operas. These were *Der Protagonist* on a libretto by the
playwright Georg Kaiser, first given at Dresden under Fritz
Busch in 1926; *Der Zar lässt sich photographieren* ('The Tsar has
himself photographed'), also on a text by Kaiser (Leipzig,
1928); and *Royal Palace* on a libretto by the expressionist poet
Iwan Goll (Kroll Oper, 1927). All three have been revived
during the past twenty years. The two Kaiser operas were
seen at Frankfort in 1960, the Iwan Goll piece at the 1971
Holland Festival. For this last revival the orchestral score was
'reconstructed' by Gunther Schuller and Noam Sheriff, and
the conductor was Gary Bertini, who has recorded the two
Weill Symphonies. *Royal Palace* is a fantasy opera not unlike
those of Schreker, and it cannot be called a success, though the
music is never uninteresting. But in these and other early
works Weill does not seem to have found a characteristic style
for himself. The music is curiously faceless.

Then he met Bertolt Brecht, known at the time as plain
Bert. David Drew has said that it was 'a mere chance of
history' that Weill's best-known works remain those which he
wrote in collaboration with Brecht. I do not agree, and feel,
like Peter Heyworth,* that Brecht's catalytic influence was
crucial in Weill's development. Without Brecht, Weill was
inclined to lapse into sentimentality—a sentimentality which
became highly marketable in his American years. His Brecht
collaborations have a toughness and virility rather lacking
elsewhere in his output.

* *The Observer*, 23 January, 1972.

Weill is normally considered to have 'found himself' with the composition of the Brecht work *Das kleine Mahagonny* (Baden-Baden, 1927). The story of the six years between this and the last Brecht creation, *Die sieben Todsünden* (1933), is the record of a highly successful attempt to evolve a homogeneous style from disparate elements—a style capable of accommodating the expression of a wide range of emotions, not only those most commonly associated with Weill: cynical nostalgia, fatigue, regret. It was a style well suited to treating the modern, social, political subjects he and the writers he worked with favoured. It was welded from neoclassical counterpoint, popular song, jazz rhythms, traces of romantic opera; and out of this unlikely mixture Weill achieved complete consistency and individuality. All but two of the major works of this period were written for the theatre, and even the two exceptions are of essentially dramatic conception: one is a radio work and one a dramatic cantata on poems by Brecht.

It was in spring 1927 that Weill finished his settings of the five Mahagonny-songs in Brecht's book of poems *Hauspostille* ('Family Prayer Book'), an ironic title, it goes without saying. Since the word *Mahagonny* will figure large in the next pages it is well to explain what Brecht meant by it. Mahagonny was a mythical city, set, supposedly, on the Florida Gold Coast, as chic as the French Riviera, rich as only an American city could be, and as full of vice and sin as Weimar Berlin. It was a *Netzestadt*, a city of nets: nets into which gullible victims could be drawn and bled for what one could get out of them. In a real sense it *was* Berlin in the 1920s, with its displays of ill-gotten wealth, its depths of wretchedness, its political instability, its latent and often open violence, its drug addiction and its flaunted transvestism and homosexuality. From Brecht's point of view it was thoroughly reprehensible, but it was a magnet for wolves and lambs. Brecht loved at this time to use American place names as mythological symbols— Pensacola, Memphis, San Francisco, even Baltimore—for America at that time seemed larger than life in every regard. As known in Europe through books, papers and the cinema, it was the country of jazz, gangsters, hurricanes, wealth, the Wild West, the Gold Rush, the electric chair. It was glamour personified. Needless to say, Brecht's America was very

different from the real thing, just as the Asia of Tristan Klingsor
and Ravel was not intended as an accurate picture. It was a
fantasy America, except in one very important regard:
America was the supreme headquarters of the economic
system Brecht never ceased to attack, the capitalist system.
And it was what Brecht saw as the evils of this system which
came under violent assault in the *Little Mahagonny* and the
full-length opera which was to incorporate it, *The Rise and
Fall of the City of Mahagonny*.

As we have noted (p. 80) *Das kleine Mahagonny* received
its first performance at the Baden-Baden contemporary music
festival in July 1927. Its companions in the quadruple bill
were more or less what the audience expected, apart, perhaps,
from the Milhaud spoof. But *Das kleine Mahagonny* took the
audience completely by surprise. The set was a boxing ring,
the sleazy low-life atmosphere was completely new, and so
was the music, which combined Handelian and Bachian
elements with deliberately popular tunes, the most famous of
which was the *Alabama-Song*, 'Oh, show us the way to the next
whisky-bar!' This, like the *Benares-Lied*, with its despondent
cries of 'Is here no telephone?', made use of the curious
'basic English' which Brecht had devised for songs such as these.
Brecht did not use only American names for exotic effect: he
also drew on India and the East Indies—the title of the well-
known song *Sorabaya-Jonny*, from *Happy End*, is a case in point.
Das kleine Mahagonny was received with cheers and boos.
Lotte Lenya tells of going into a hotel afterwards and finding
members of the audience engaged in animated discussion
about the new work. Then someone slapped her on the back
and boomed 'Is here no telephone?' It was Otto Klemperer.

This was the first Brecht-Weill creation to reveal to the
musical public the brilliant talent of Lenya, Weill's wife,
whose voice was later to remind Margot Oxford and Asquith
of 'a disillusioned child singing outside a public house'. She
was to score perhaps the greatest success of her career in one
of the two Brecht works which delayed somewhat Weill's
expansion of the *Little Mahagonny* into the full-length opera
which developed from it. These two works were *Die Dreigroschenoper* ('The Threepenny Opera') and *Happy End*, the latter
a flop, the former an enormous success, whose staging (again

with Lenya) at the Theater de Lys in New York in 1954 heralded the Weill revival.

The Threepenny Opera was commissioned by the producer Ernst-Josef Aufricht, who presented it at the Theater am Schiffbauerdamm in Berlin on 31 August, 1928. As is well known, it was a reworking in 'modern' terms of *The Beggar's Opera*, by John Gay. The setting was Soho, presented, plausibly enough, as a world of thieves, whores, ponces and corrupt policemen. But it was not a twentieth-century Soho. It was, on the contrary, the same nineteenth-century London, evil, sinister and swathed in fog, which formed the setting for the death of Alban Berg's 'heroine' Lulu at the hands of Jack the Ripper and which had fascinated French writers in Victorian times. But it was also Berlin. The German capital was being offered a distorting mirror of itself. And Berlin loved it. There is little to suggest that either Brecht or Weill attached as much importance to *The Threepenny Opera* as they did to other projects on which they were engaged, but the work was a runaway success. This was due more to Weill than to Brecht, for the audience loved the tunes more than the satire. It seems that the poet had not originally envisaged a musical contribution as extensive as his collaborator provided. Not that it is a large-scale work in musical terms: it is most ingeniously scored for a mere eight players, who between them play flute, two clarinets, bassoon, two saxophones, trumpet, trombone, piano, harmonium, banjo, guitar, piano accordion, percussion, 'cello and double-bass. Weill used only one of the tunes from the original *Beggar's Opera:* that originally set to the words 'Through all the employments of life' and now re-named *Peachum's Morning Chorale.* Weill invented haunting tunes of his own—*Seeräuber Jenny* ('Pirate Jenny'), the *Barbara song*, the tango duet in which Jenny betrays Mackie Messer (Macheath, renamed), and of course the famous *Moritat*, which, as 'Mack the Knife', has gone round the world. Some of the work's successes have been scored in unlikely places. When the Nazis opened what they called a 'Museum of Degenerate Art' at Nuremberg, they devoted a room to Weill, with a record player dispensing his music. So popular did this become with people coming to hear their favourite tunes— tunes they no longer dared play at home—that the Nazis

were obliged to close the room down. Weill's songs display
what Virgil Thomson, writing, with his usual percipience, in
1933, called 'a perfection of prosody unequalled by any other
European composer' (of the day).

Happy End, which followed on 2 September, 1929, at the
same theatre, was an attempt to repeat the success of *The
Threepenny Opera*, though on this occasion Brecht contributed
only the lyrics. A story of gangsters and molls in Chicago, it
tried to exploit the fascination of 'low life', as the earlier work
had done. On the first night an actress in the cast created a
certain amount of disruption by suddenly beginning to read
from a political pamphlet, but in the main things went well
until the finale, whose tone, strongly opposed to the Right
and to religion, created much offence among press and public.
The result was complete failure. In any case *Happy End* lacks
the strength, conviction and consistency of its predecessor and
it seems unlikely that it could ever have achieved a comparable
success, disruption or no disruption. It contains however some
superb songs, such as the *Bilbao-Song* ('Bill's Dance Hall in
Bilbao'), the *Sailor-Tango* and, best of all, the famous *Sorabaya-
Jonny*, arguably Weill's finest essay in this particular vein and
for ever associated with the voice of Lotte Lenya, though she
was not in the original cast of the production.

During this period Weill had been working on his expansion
of *Das kleine Mahagonny* into the full-length opera which he
called *Aufstieg und Fall der Stadt Mahagonny* ('The Rise and Fall
of the City of Mahagonny'). This was finished in 1929 and
received its first performance at the Neue Theater in Leipzig
on 9 March, 1930, in a production staged by Walter Brügmann,
designed by Caspar Neher, and conducted by Gustav Brecher.
At the premiere the theatre was surrounded by Brownshirts
protesting against the work. Lenya, who was in the audience,
has described the tension inside the theatre. Towards the end
of the opera a demonstration started, grew in violence and
eventually spread to the stage. Police arrived and cleared the
house. The city council considered cancelling further performances, and, though they decided against it, the second
took place with the house lights on and police in the theatre
from the start.

For another reason—a purely musical one—the work did

not enjoy at Leipzig the success it deserved. The work had been cast, naturally enough, from the members of the opera company, but *Mahagonny* demanded something rather different, as will be seen when the nature of the work is discussed. It needed a cast of singing actors. Technically the roles of the soloists demanded stronger, more schooled voices than the leading parts in *The Threepenny Opera*, but they also asked for more histrionic ability than the average opera singer possessed.

It was therefore not until the opera was produced in Berlin that it revealed itself as the masterpiece it is. The producer Ernst-Josef Aufricht (who had commissioned *The Threepenny Opera*) presented *Mahagonny* there in December 1931, taking over the Kurfürstendamm-Theater from Max Reinhardt for the purpose. For the production Aufricht made changes in both stage and auditorium, and he cast the work with singing actors—Lenya as Jenny, Harald Paulsen as the hero, Jimmy Mahoney, and Trude Hesterberg as Widow Begbick, the creator and animator of the city of Mahagonny. Aufricht's intention was to present the opera for a commercial run in the theatre, and its success with the discriminating Berlin audience was great. But the National Socialists, growing ever more powerful, attacked the work as 'degenerate' and 'culturally Bolshevist', and it was denied the commercial triumph that ought to have accompanied its artistic success. Nor has it been very fortunate in its revivals. It has never made much impact in America, though an excellent recording exists. In England, on the other hand, it was staged at Sadler's Wells Theatre in London under Colin Davis (first performance of the new production: 16 January, 1963) and received, on the whole, rapturously. It is overdue for revival.

Aufstieg und Fall der Stadt Mahagonny is possibly Weill's greatest work. Its only rivals would seem to be *Die Sieben Todsünden* ('The Seven Deadly Sins') and, perhaps, *Die Bürgschaft* ('The Pledge'). Its mixture of styles is as heady as that in *Jonny spielt auf*, but the opera coheres, which is a remarkable achievement, given the ingredients. There is, first of all, the 'song' element: strophic songs, often in Brecht's strange pidgin English, with accompaniments that are basically simple though decorated ingeniously. There are polyphonic passages for orchestra, or for chorus and orchestra, clearly and intelligently derived from models of the baroque era but in no way pastiches. In the great 'Crane Duet' for Jenny and Jimmy the treatment is canonic in style, the sound transparent and pure. H. H. Stuckenschmidt has pointed to the reminiscence at one point in the work of the duet for the two Men in Armour in *Die Zauberflöte;* this occurs in the figured chorale *Haltet euch aufrecht* ('Hold yourselves upright'). He also claims to see a parody of the Bridesmaids' Chorus from *Der Freischütz* in the male quartet *Auf nach Mahagonny!* There are many other ingredients: nineteenth-century salon music, popular German (as opposed to American) song, chorales, tangos.

The work is scored for an orchestra of thirty, capable of sounding now like a jazz band, now like a small classical orchestra. Wind and percussion are emphasised, and the instruments include banjo, bass guitar, piano, harmonium, accordion, zither and saxophone. There are three acts and twenty-one musical sections, each introduced by a Speaker, who sets the scene, brings the action up to date or announces the theme of the scene to come.

After a tense contrapuntal prelude, the curtain rises. A battered truck comes on stage, and stops. It contains three people. They will be the founders of the city. They are Leokadja Begbick, a dominating and utterly unscrupulous widow, and her assistants Dreieinigkeit Moses ('Trinity Moses') and Fatty the Bookkeeper. The Speaker has already told us that they are fugitives from justice and that the police are after them. The truck has not simply stopped: it has broken down. There is nothing to be done but found a city then and there. There is gold on the coast, but getting gold from the earth is a troublesome business: the rivers are reluctant to yield their riches. Far easier, says Widow Begbick, to obtain gold from men. In high baroque style (a style which Weill's admirer and translator Marc Blitzstein was to echo in the pronouncements of that other female ogre, Regina, in his opera of that name) the Widow announces her intention of founding a city to be called Mahagonny, the 'city of nets'—nets for birds, or rather for gulls. It will offer ease, comfort, prize-fights, gin and whisky, women and boys: everything a man could want. There, anyone may do as he wishes. As the flag of the city is hoisted on a fishing rod, the founders sing that it exists only because everything is evil, because there is no peace and harmony to be found anywhere, and there is nothing on which man can rely.

In the next few weeks, says the Speaker, the first sharks begin to arrive. Jenny and six other girls come on to the stage, carrying suitcases. They sit down on them and embark on the *Alabama-Song*, 'Oh, show us the way to the next whisky-bar!' They have lost their Good Old Mamma, they say; and so they must have whisky, pretty boys and dollars: especially dollars.

The next section brings a complete change of mood and style. It provides one of many striking instances of Weill's power of effortless transition. The fame of Mahagonny has started to spread. Behind the scenes the men of the cities are heard singing of the drabness and tedium of their life. Below the cities are sewers; above them is smoke; in them is . . . nothing. The style of this chorus comes straight from that old strong, dark German tradition which runs through Buxtehude to Bach and the more 'German' works of Mozart. There is an austerely dignified sadness at the words *Wir vergehen rasch, und langsam vergehen sie auch* ('We perish quickly and slowly they too will perish'). Fatty and Moses appear to extol the delights of the 'golden city', where calm reigns and the drinks are cheap. Their praise and promotion of the city they have founded mingle with the chorus of the city-dwellers. Again Fatty and Moses urge them to come to Mahagonny: only yesterday people there were asking about them.

The first sharks have arrived; now the first birds to be drawn into the net make their appearance. They are lumber-men from Alaska: Jimmy Mahoney, Jakob Schmidt (known as Jake), Sparbüchsenbill ('Pennybank-Bill') and the splendidly-named Alaska-Wolf-Joe. The Speaker says that they represent the discontented of all the continents. They sing a raucously jazzy number, *Auf nach Mahagonny!*, with a refrain begging the 'beautiful green moon of Alabama' to shine on them. It is this passage which has the air of a parody of the *Bridesmaids' Chorus*. They have plenty of money, earned in seven years of freezing cold in Alaska. Now they are in a mood to spend it on pleasure.

They are greeted by Widow Begbick, who arrives with a long list and checks off each man's personal tastes, to an ironical and rather sinister orchestral accompaniment. It is at once clear that Jimmy does not like her. Obviously, the men want girls. Trinity Moses sets out various pictures from which they may choose, but Jimmy demands to see the real thing. The girls appear—Jenny and her six colleagues. Jake is unwilling to pay fifty dollars for Jenny. She sings the *Havana-Lied*, another number associated indelibly with the voice of Lotte Lenya. It has suggestions of jazz as well as a suitably Latin American flavour. Jenny sings that her mother once warned her never to sell her body for just a few dollars: think it over, Mr Jakob Schmidt, she says. Jake lowers his offer to twenty dollars. But Jenny has caught Jimmy's interest. He will take her, he says. He tells her his wishes, and asks to know what hers are; she replies evasively. In their exchanges there is a strange mixture of tender lyricism and frankly commercial eroticism. Or perhaps it is strange only to those who think that any kind of tenderness is *necessarily* absent from a sexual relationship which is *au fond* based on the transfer of money from one hand to another.

All is not well: Mahagonny is not turning out to be such good business after all. Widow Begbick suggests abandoning the city and returning whence they came. This is not possible, says Fatty, for the sheriffs have been looking for her at Pensacola. There is nothing for it but to stay, hoping that more people with money will be lured to Mahagonny. The scene includes a curious and sleazy passage in which the Widow recalls her own amorous adventures, standing against a wall with a man and talking of love. But the money, she says, is gone, and sexual desire went with it. In this work, and elsewhere in Brecht at this time, sex and money are always closely associated.

Jimmy is discontented and rebellious; he wants to leave. His friends try to dissuade him: the gin and whisky are cheap, there is peace, you can smoke, you can sleep. Why should he want to go? True, says Jimmy, but there is something missing: *Aber etwas fehlt.* He embarks on a number which encapsulates boredom: *Ich glaube, ich will meinen Hut aufessen* ('I think I'm going to eat my hat'). At the end of each stanza his friends ridicule his state of mind. As they do so, the music becomes more animated, only to sag again at Jimmy's repeated words

Ich will doch gar kein Mensch sein ('I don't want to be a human
being'). But in the end he allows himself to be led back to
Mahagonny.

The next scene begins in an atmosphere of treacherous
calm. The men of Mahagonny are sitting outside the 'Here-
You-May-Do-Anything-Inn', smoking, drinking and listening
to a 'rendering' of *The Maiden's Prayer* on a pub piano. 'That is
eternal art', says Jake. Jim, moved, embarks on a highly
emotional, not to say maudlin, reminiscence of the life he and
his friends used to live in Alaska among the snow forests,
through the seven winters of privation which enabled them to
accumulate the money they are now spending. As Jimmy
begins to work himself up into a rage, the music too develops
into a complicated finale to the scene in which Widow Begbick,
Fatty, Moses, the girls, the four men and the men of Mahagonny
(represented by the chorus) all participate. At the end Jimmy
leaps on to the table and, to the music that ended the scene
of the founding of the city, sings that no one will ever be happy
in Mahagonny because there is too much peace, too much
harmony, and too much on which one can depend.

Now comes one of the most superb pages in the whole score.
The Speaker announces that Mahagonny is threatened not
only by internal discontents: a peril is on the way from outside.
A hurricane is bearing down on the city. A harshly magni-
ficent fugato passage dominated by wind instruments leads into
the chorus *O furchtbares Ereignis!* ('Oh terrible event!'), in
which the inhabitants of the city presage its destruction. Their
hushed appeals—'Where is there a wall to hide me? Where is
there a cave to receive me?'—recall the choruses of the Bach
Passions. The form of this comparatively short piece—fugal
introduction on winds, choral lamentation, choral cries for
help, lamentation again and return to the instrumental
introduction—is perfectly satisfying, and the classical economy
of its rendition of abject panic is masterly. It outclasses
attempts in a similar idiom in Honegger's admittedly fine
Le Roi David.

There follows the night of the hurricane. All are in despair.
Only Jim smiles: he has found the law of human happiness—
do everything that you want. Man destroys all that exists: no
hurricane can equal the destructiveness of man in search of

amusement. The men of Mahagonny intone the chorale *Haltet euch aufrecht;* the girls sing melancholy snatches of the *Alabama-Song;* Jim philosophises. Meanwhile the hurricane destroys Pensacola, killing righteous and unrighteous alike. Among the former are the sheriffs who are in search of Widow Begbick, and even in her fear she finds time to rejoice at their downfall. The lights dim: all that is visible now is a projection of a map with an arrow that moves slowly towards Mahagonny, indicating the path of the hurricane. Curtain.

At the beginning of the Second Act nothing has changed: the typhoon has now destroyed Atsena and is continuing its course towards the City of Nets. Then, suddenly, it makes a detour. Mahagonny has been spared. In a brief and beautiful chorus, very lightly accompanied, the chorus give thanks.

Now, in their relief at being spared, the population of Mahagonny turn to every possible form of self-indulgence. This is symbolished in the opera by eating, drinking, boxing-matches and sex, all carried as far as it is possible to go.

First comes a scene in which Jake literally eats himself to death, to the accompaniment of a slow waltz, with on-stage accordion and zither. Squalider still, if possible, is the following scene, when the men 'turn to love' and are seen queueing up to take their turn with a girl. As they wait, they sing a quietly urgent song, bidding the man currently with the girl to hurry up: the moon is going down, and 'it will not always shine over you, Mandalay'. This introduction, not for the first time in the opera, of a reference to Mandalay is typical of Brecht: he liked the name, it sounded exotic, and he had no qualms about throwing it in alongside Alabama, Pensacola and the rest. Nor should one forget Brecht's acknowledged debt to Rudyard Kipling.

There is now an astonishing transformation of mood, from squalor to lyricism of the most poignant and pure kind. As the brothel music fades, Jimmy and Jenny are seen sitting together, he smoking, she making herself up. They sing the so-called 'Crane Duet', *Sieh jene Kraniche in grossem Bogen* ('Look at those cranes sweeping wide'), in which two cranes, flying together, totally lost in each other, symbolise two lovers, briefly together, soon to be parted: *So scheint die Liebe Liebenden ein Halt* ('So love to lovers seems a stop in time'). The two

voices pursue their cool way over a quiet accompaniment
dominated by woodwind instruments, until, after a series of
questions and answers, put by Jimmy, answered by Jenny,
the music ends majestically and tragically with a passage which
wonderfully conveys the vulnerability and fragility of love
and of lovers.

The next scene is a boxing-match, with a brass band playing
suitably coarse music. Joe is to fight Trinity Moses. Jim, at
the ringside, and Joe, in the ring, recall their days together in
Alaska. Jim puts all his remaining money on Joe; Bill, more
prudent, takes a look at the two contestants and holds back.
He is wise, for Trinity Moses knocks Joe out and kills him. At
the referee's announcement *Der Mann ist tot!* Brecht asks for
a great and continuing burst of laughter. It is one of the most
shocking moments in the whole work.

In despair, Jim invites everyone to drink with him. He gets
very drunk himself, and announces his intention of going back
to Alaska. He takes the billiard-table for a ship. The others
enter into the spirit of the thing, and imagine themselves
sailing through perilous seas, the music quoting the German
popular song *Stürmisch die Nacht*. But the dream is shattered
when Moses appears, wanting the money for the drinks. It is
not Alaska after all: still Mahagonny. Jimmy cannot pay.
Jenny refuses to help: why should she? As the men tie Jimmy
up, Jenny walks backwards and forwards along the footlights,
delivering the song *Wie man sich bettet*: 'For as you make your
bed, so must you lie on it'. She reveals her philosophy of life:
'If someone's going to kick, it'll be me; and if someone's
going to be kicked, it'll be you.'

Jim is waiting for the dawn. In an austere, despairing tango,
he prays that the day will never come: but it does. This
movement found an echo later in the tangos of Virgil Thomson,
notably in his music for the Lorentz film *The Plow That Broke
the Plains*. The extreme economy of Weill's scoring was a
lesson well learned by Thomson. The Second Act ends at this
point.

The savagery of the trial scene surpasses even that of the
boxing-match. Moses, prosecuting attorney, is seen selling
tickets: only five dollars, he says, to see justice in action. One
Toby Higgins is accused of premeditated murder, indulged

in simply for the sake of trying out an old revolver. But Higgins
produces money, no injured party comes forward (*Die Toten
reden nicht*—'Dead men tell no tales') and he is acquitted. They
turn their attention to Jimmy. In sentimental German romantic
style, Jim asks Bill for money to help him conduct his case
'humanely'. In music equally sentimental, Bill turns him
down: he feels close to Jimmy as a person, he says, but money
is another matter altogether. The trial proceeds. Jimmy is
accused of various crimes, by far the worst of which is his lack
of money. There is a stunned silence at his words *Ich habe kein
Geld*. To be penniless is the worst crime on the face of the earth:
and it is because Jimmy is penniless that he is condemned to
death. Brecht's ferocious hatred of injustice shines out in the
whole episode.

There follows the *Benares-Lied*. The Speaker introduces it
by saying that there were now many people in Mahagonny
who longed for another, better town, called Benares. But
Benares was destroyed by an earthquake. This is another
song in Brechtian English:

> There is no whisky in this town.
> There is no bar to sit us down.
> Oh!
> Where is the telephone?
> Oh!
> Is here no telephone?
> Oh sir, God help me, no . . .

It is, I suppose, possible to find this song 'quaint', 'funny',
'amusing'. That would perhaps be an understandable reaction.
Indeed I confess that it was my reaction the first time I heard
it. Closer acquaintance with the song teaches one better. It
is like the maudlin singing of drunks in a pub just before
closing time. Its atmosphere recalls the famous passage at the
end of 'A Game of Chess' in *The Waste Land*, with its repeated
'Hurry up please it's time'. It conveys a feeling of total despair.
Brecht's characters are quite lost. They have not the slightest
idea of what to do or where to go. The high string descant at
the words 'There is not much fun on this star' is unbearably
poignant, as is the final repetition of the question 'Where
shall we go?' The song is an extraordinary musical invention.

Jimmy, awaiting execution, sings a stoic farewell to life, in which he denies belief in any sort of immortality. Man is an animal, and dies like an animal, never to live again in any form. The mood grows blacker and blacker. Seated in the electric chair, Jimmy asks Widow Begbick whether she does not know that there is a God. She has an answer ready: she bids the men stage the play about God in Mahagonny (*Das Spiel von Gott in Mahagonny*). This, naturally, is a passage which gave much offence at the premiere and thereafter. While Jimmy's execution proceeds, the men act out a play in which God appears *mitten in Whisky* ('in the midst of whisky') to reproach the inhabitants of Mahagonny for their misdeeds. He orders them down to hell. But they will not go: they are in hell already. The piece builds to a great climax in which amid the clangour of bells the men of Mahagonny reject God once and for all.

Against a background of Mahagonny in flames, processions march across the stage, bearing placards with contradictory slogans. The cost of living has risen to ridiculous proportions. The city is in the process of destruction. Jimmy's personal possessions are carried in procession like the relics of a saint. The music recalls earlier sections of the opera—*Wie man sich bettet*, the *Alabama-Song*, the night of the hurricane, the foundation of the city—and finally resolves itself into the shattering chorus *Können einem toten Mann nicht helfen*. You cannot help a dead man, sing the chorus. You cannot help anyone. Their message is punctuated with slashing chords that bring the opera to its close with a feeling of absolute finality.

This masterpiece had no large progeny. Weill abandoned such enterprises in the 1930s. It is only in the work of Marc Blitzstein that one can detect an influence stemming from *Mahagonny*, and this fact will not be well understood until *Mahagonny* is better known in both Britain and the U.S. and British listeners acquire at least a little familiarity with the work of Blitzstein. At present, unhappily, this important American composer is to all intents and purposes unknown in Britain. His powerful musical drama *Regina*, based on the play *The Little Foxes*, by Lilian Hellman, has more than a little in common with *Mahagonny*, though it is not of comparable originality and lacks quite the shattering power of Weill's work. Yet it packs a remarkable musical and theatrical punch which are apparent from a mere acquaintance with the (excellent) recording. Mention has already been made of the resemblance between the masterful Handelian quality of the recitatives allotted to the monstrous Regina and those given to Leocadja Begbick. But there are other connections too. Blitzstein shows an eclecticism similar to Weill's, and if *Regina* is not quite so masterful as *Mahagonny* in integrating its various elements it certainly achieves a very fair degree of success. Blitzstein juggles with Handelian recitative, jazz, negro spiritual, patterns derived from Broadway musicals, romantic dance music of the nineteenth century, 'Deep South' romanticism, grandiloquent classicism.

Blitzstein's death in a car accident in Martinique in January 1964 was a serious loss. It deprived the world of a projected opera about Sacco and Vanzetti, the two Italian immigrants executed for allegedly murdering a guard during a robbery in Massachusetts in the 1920s. The Sacco and Vanzetti case was a *cause celèbre* of the left and inspired Ben Shahn to painting as well as Blitzstein to music. Blitzstein resembled Weill not only in his Jewishness but also in his political stance. The Sacco and Vanzetti opera was a Ford Foundation commission, and was to have been presented at the Metropolitan Opera House. Two acts of the work were later found in the boot of Blitzstein's car, and it was given out that Leonard Bernstein, who had known Blitzstein, was to complete the work. But nothing further has been heard. Perhaps it proved impracticable, or perhaps Mr Bernstein has been too busy with television appearances, radical chic, conducting the New York and Vienna orchestras and scaling the heights (or plumbing the depths, whichever way it strikes you) with the *Mass* to devote any time to his late *confrère*.

Before dealing with what might be called Weill's last important 'German' work (though it was first given elsewhere) one should mention some of his other compositions before Hitler's rise to power forced him to leave Germany for ever.

I do not propose to dwell on the radio cantata *Der Lindberghflug*, which was originally to have been a collaboration with Paul Hindemith, but which in the end Weill completed on his own. Despite the advocacy of Colin Davis, it strikes me as one of Weill's dullest efforts. Likewise the cantata *Das Berliner Requiem* (first heard in a Frankfort Radio broadcast on 22 May, 1929) does not seem to me to represent its composer at his best, apart from the section *Vom ertrunkenen Mädchen* ('Concerning a drowned girl'), whose words and music are both lovely and which sounds much better in the simplicity of Lotte Lenya's recording than in its original version.

Der Jasager (1930) is a strange and distasteful piece, though the distastefulness lies not in the music but in the text. This was a 'school-opera' by Brecht, designed for performance by amateurs. It relates to Hindemith's work in this area, though it possesses more musical interest than any of Hindemith's pieces for amateur performers. It also anticipates Weill's later 'student opera', written in America, *Down in the Valley*, though that was as soft as *Der Jasager* was hard. *Der Jasager* was a *Lehrstück*, a didactic piece, designed to instruct rather than to entertain, but its lesson is a particularly pernicious one. It has been given two fairly recent revivals in Britain, one at the Edinburgh Festival of 1974 and one by the Leicestershire Schools Symphony Orchestra, under the direction of Alexander Goehr. One hopes that the children were not infected by the opera's ideas.

Der Jasager is based on a Nō-play, called *Taniko* or *The Valley Hurling*. It is the story of a group of children who go under the supervision of a teacher to see a wise man who lives beyond the mountains. The boy-hero pleads to go with them, because he wishes to obtain medicine for his sick mother in the distant town which is the children's goal. It is a hard journey, and he cannot keep up with the others. He is told that it is the custom in such cases for the failing member of the party to be left behind to die, so that the expedition shall not be impeded. The boy consents to be left, but asks to be killed at once rather than have to suffer a slow death. His companions obligingly hurl him over the cliff. Having done so, they proceed. It is an extraordinarily nasty work, though in fairness to Brecht it should be added that in response to criticism from pupils at the schools which had performed the work he rewrote the piece as *Der Neinsager*. Yet it would be unfair to Weill to allow distaste for the 'message' of *Der*

Jasager (one which could appeal only to a totalitarian-minded audience; in fact, ironically, the work was seen by some at the time as an attempt to inculcate the virtues of 'Prussian' discipline) to affect judgment of the music. Ned Rorem, for one, has put on record his very high opinion of the piece. The music is deliberately simple, but it can be moving, notably in the conversation between the teacher and the boy which precedes the latter's act of voluntary self-immolation. But the mechanistic march-rhythms of the close have for me the unpleasant effect that some (though not I) find in the *Carmina Burana* of Carl Orff.

For two major works Weill turned for libretti to other writers than Brecht. The designer Caspar Neher provided him with a text for his ambitious opera *Die Bürgschaft* (Berlin, 1932). This is clearly a very substantial piece but one on which I hesitate to comment at all, never having heard a bar of it played. David Drew thinks highly of it, but proper appraisal must await performance.

Der Silbersee ('The Silver Lake'), on the other hand, was revived at the 1971 Holland Festival in a concert version made by Drew and Josef Heinzelmann; Gary Bertini conducted and Lotte Lenya participated in the performance as Narrator, also taking one of the characters, Frau von Luber. The words were by the expressionist playwright who had provided earlier libretti for Weill, Georg Kaiser. The work, described as 'a winter legend', was in fact written in the winter of 1932–3. It appeared at a bad moment. Less than three weeks before its triple premiere (at Leipzig and two other German cities) on 18 February, 1933, Hitler finally came to power. The Reichstag burned down on 27 February. The directors of official opera houses had become progressively more reluctant to stage Weill's works, because of Nazi hostility to a composer who was both a Jew and a member of the left wing. Therefore Weill planned *Der Silbersee* as a play with much music (about seventy-five minutes of it), for actors capable of singing against an orchestra of some size. The work opened, was greeted with Nazi demonstrations, and was closed down by official edict the following day. It was the *Cäsar Ballade*, telling the story of the death of Caesar and by implication attacking all dictators, which created the greatest offence.

Weill had written a fine score, but, perhaps because of the nature of the text, it lacked the bite of his Brecht collaborations. The end, in particular, is weakly sentimental.

The final work of Weill which I wish to discuss in detail is the ballet *Die sieben Todsünden der Kleinbürger* ('The Seven Deadly Sins of the Petit-Bourgeois'), which summed up and crowned the Brecht-Weill collaboration. It looks back to the deliberate 'sleaziness' of the 1920s and forward to the politically-oriented 1930s. Brecht provided an excellent poem, which, curiously, he does not seem to have thought well of himself: his text is by turns sharp, acrid, cynical, nostalgic, weary, and always fiercely moral. It is also compact and economical. The references to exotic place-names are still present, but they are used with more point and discretion than heretofore. There is no politics, as such, but the social criticism is all the more devastating for being implied rather than driven home with a sledgehammer. Weill responded with a score which is all of a piece; it is bound together thematically in a way that is both musically satisfying and dramatically inevitable. The symmetrical shape of the libretto and the absence of spoken dialogue enabled Weill to produce a tauter, more rigorous musical work than had been possible in, for instance, *Mahagonny*, which was broken up by spoken sections and had inevitably to consist of separate numbers. But the work's production history has not been entirely happy and the problems it presents arise to some degree from its very nature, as will be seen.

It is described as a *Ballet with Song*. It is scored for a female singer, a quartet of two tenors and two basses, and an orchestra of normal size. The heroine is a certain Anna. She has a dual personality, a practical side (represented by the singer) and an idealistic side (represented by a corresponding dancer); or maybe they are two sisters—one cannot be certain. The male quartet are Anna's family, mother being represented by a booming bass. Anna and her sister come from Louisiana, where their family are attempting to build 'a little house'. It is in order to earn money to help in the building that the sisters set out on a journey that takes them through seven American cities before they return home, weary and wiser.

In the *Prologue* the basic situation is set out by the singing

Anna. This movement (the first two pages of which had the rare distinction of being printed in the first number of the *de luxe avant-garde* art magazine *Minotaure*) already has a feeling of fatigue, mingled with nostalgia for Louisiana, to which the sisters want to return as soon as they can. The music plods along as if the sisters are dragging their feet in the effort to force themselves to embark on their journey. *Meine Schwester ist schön, ich bin praktisch*, explains the singing Anna: she is the practical one. She represents the cold light of reason and common sense, the dancing Anna the natural impulses of a generous instinct. In each city Anna will be tempted by a sin, and in each her practical persona will enable her to triumph over temptation. But here the irony begins. The sins into which Anna risks falling are for the most part warm human impulses; these must be sternly suppressed in the interest not of the Christian ethic but in order to conform with petit-bourgeois 'morality'. Virtue is equated with what is commercially expedient, vice with what is commercially unwise. The work is to be a savage attack on the values of a capitalist, money-dominated society, as was *Mahagonny*.

During *Faulheit* ('Sloth'), a Tarantella, the Family, remembering that Anna always had to be hauled out of bed in the morning, express the hope that she will be industrious. The final passage is a prayer to God to 'enlighten our children that they may know the way that leads to prosperity'. This prayer, and the brief instrumental coda which rounds it off, will be heard again, the latter notably at the end of the 'Lust' movement.

Stolz auf das Beste des Ichs ('Pride') is a blowsy waltz. It finds Anna working in a cabaret in Memphis. She wants to be an artist, to create art in the cabaret, but it is nudity that the customers are after. The practical Anna manages to subdue her sister's 'pride': the clients get what they want.

Now comes *Zorn über die Gemeinheit* ('Anger'). The Family complain hotly that nothing like enough money is being sent home: the house will never get built at this rate! Anna announces that they/she have arrived at Los Angeles: as extras, they have the chance to go far in the film business. But the idealistic Anna is a nuisance: she objects to brutality (unspecified in the text, but symbolised in the original production

by cruelty to animals during filming). Again the singing
Anna manages to persuade her troublesome twin to see reason,
with the words:

> *Wer dem Unrecht in den Arm fällt,*
> *den will man nirgends haben . . .*
> *Wer da nichts verschuldet*
> *der sühnt auf Erden . . .*
>
> (He who tries to stop injustice
> Is not wanted anywhere . . .
> He who does no wrong
> Will atone for it on earth . . .')

The second and longer part of this section is a Shimmy-
Foxtrot. For sheer hopelessness it would be hard to match the
movement's final statement of the theme to which the above
words are set: it is sung by the strings with a horn descant
against a chattering, repetitive jazz accompaniment on woodwind and brass, to be finally halted by an abrupt banjo chord.
It surely represents the aching awareness of the gradually
'maturing' idealistic Anna that an enormous gulf exists
between her natural human impulses and the courses of action
society requires of her if she is to 'succeed'.

Comedy, at least on the surface, follows. In barber-shop
harmonies the dreadful Family tell that they have received a
letter from Philadelphia. Anna has been contracted as a solo
dancer, provided she keeps her weight down. That is going to
be a problem, for Anna is a greedy girl. She must suppress
her Gluttony (*Völlerei*): no one wants hippopotamuses in
Philadelphia. The Family express their alarm at the thought
of the daily weighing their daughter is going to have to
undergo: woe if she has gained even an ounce! They console
themselves with the thought that Anna will be a sensible girl
and content herself with dreaming of all the extremely fatten-
ing goodies she can eat when she finally returns to the little
house in Louisiana. Much of this movement is for the male
quartet with the lightest of guitar accompaniments, but at
the words *Aber Anna ist ja sehr verständig* ('But Anna is very
reasonable') the music changes, with deliberately ridiculous
effect, into a romantic tenor solo with a plucked string

accompaniment, the Family echoing the tenor's naming of each delightful titbit that will await Anna's return. In this movement, though, as in other Brecht-Weill inspirations, there is a basic seriousness below the superficial comedy: the tenor passage and its sequel are moving as well as funny.

The mood changes to near-tragedy in the next movement, *Unzucht* ('Lust'), set, of all places, in Boston. This displays to particular advantage the qualities of Brecht's marvellously sinewy text and Weill's imaginative response to it. Anna has found a lover who pays well for her favours. But, alas, she has fallen in love elsewhere. Worse still, she gives money to the man she loves. This, of course, is highly immoral. The practical Anna breaks the second relationship up: indeed she herself meets Fernando, the penniless lover, several times. But there was never anything between them—too ridiculous! (The expression which Lotte Lenya gets into the word *Lächerlich* is extraordinarily amusing.) The tragic style of the opening, sleazy and jazz-influenced, changes appropriately to a passage in which the music becomes seductively erotic while the words remain harshly realistic. The final section, when the practical Anna describes her sister crying in the night after she has been parted from her lover, is most moving.

Habsucht bei Raub und Betrug ('Covetousness') again features the Family, this time in a fast waltz. They hope that Anna will not be *too* covetous: avarice is an excellent thing, but it must be controlled, and a little judicious charity here and there does no harm.

The final sin is *Neid auf die Glücklichen* ('Envy'). The sisters reach San Francisco. After the Introduction, a single musical phrase, savagely repeated six times, denotes the appearance before Anna of visions of the six previous 'sins', the natural desires she has contrived somehow to suppress. She experiences regret, and feels envy for those who, unlike her, have given in to their natural impulses. In a stern march her sister reproaches her: self-control is all, for it brings prosperity. Without it no one can triumph. Not for the first time, one can hear how much the music of Mahler influenced Weill.

In the *Finaletto* the sisters return to Louisiana. The little house has been finished. The music returns to the slow tread of the beginning, and the sisters seem to sink back into the womb of the Family. The end is full of heartache, but it is in no way sentimental. It is as if Anna is shutting her eyes with relief after the exertions of a long journey in which she has been obliged, in the interests of 'morality', to suppress every good and human instinct she has ever known.

The work received its first performance at the Théâtre des Champs-Elysées in Paris on 7 June, 1933. It was presented by *Les Ballets 1933*, the company founded by the Englishman Edward James, with Boris Kochno as artistic director. (The whole enterprise of the *Ballets 1933* will be discussed on pp. 128–30). Caspar Neher, Weill's frequent collaborator, designed the sets and costumes. Balanchine was responsible for the choreography. Lenya was the singing Anna, Tilly Losch the dancing Anna. The conductor was Maurice de Abravanel, who (like Claudio Arrau) had been a composition pupil of Weill's in Berlin.

There were problems in staging the ballet. Brecht, who, like Weill, had now left Germany, was not in Paris but in Denmark. As will be seen from the synopsis, the story is not an easy one to tell in balletic terms. The moral is a hard one for ballet to convey. Brecht's text lacked stage directions of any kind. Some episodes—like *Pride* and *Lust*—made it quite clear what stage action was required to accompany the text. Others— for instance *Sloth* and *Anger*—required the invention of suitable episodes to illustrate the sins in action. Edward James and Boris Kochno, to whom the scenario was credited, devised these episodes. Neher designed seven doors, one for each sin, each papered up; when Anna passed through each she tore the paper. The real trouble was—and remains—the fact that the work is really quite self-sufficient as a concert or radio cantata, provided the words can be clearly understood. In truth, stage action is not needed at all. One sympathises therefore to some degree with the choreographers who have had to grapple with what is in fact a problem incapable of satisfactory solution.

The Paris audience was sharply divided in its reaction. Weill and his wife were staying in Paris as house guests of Charles and Marie-Laure de Noailles. Janet Flanner, writing about the opening, said that it was the most fashionable gathering she had seen in a Paris theatre since the *Soirées de*

Paris, and noticed that Weill took his cheers and boos standing in the paper door marked *Luxure* ('Lust').* The production was seen briefly, shortly afterwards, at the Savoy Theatre in London, where it was renamed *Anna-Anna*, presumably lest English audiences, not yet inured to Brecht by the doughty efforts of Martin Esslin and Kenneth Tynan, might be put off by a title like *The Seven Deadly Sins of the Petit-Bourgeois*. It was not much liked. Shortly after, the company ceased to exist.

There was a production in Copenhagen, with new choreography by Harald Lander, in 1936, but this was withdrawn almost immediately because of political pressure from Berlin. When the 'Weill revival' in the U.S. began in the 1950s, Balanchine produced the work with his own company, the New York City Ballet (4 December, 1958). W. H. Auden and Chester Kallman made a clumsy translation of Brecht's text, and the new sets were the work of Rouben Ter-Arutunian. Lenya sang, Allegra Kent danced Anna. The revival enjoyed a certain success but did not hold its place in the repertory. Once again the problem of the redundancy of the dance element had defied resolution.

Worse was to befall the work in Britain. Kenneth Macmillan produced his own version for the 1961 Edinburgh Festival (and in recent years it has been taken in modified form into the repertory of the Royal Ballet). The intention had been that the two Annas should be Anya Linden and Lotte Lenya, but Lenya disapproved of the style of the production, pleaded ill health, and withdrew. She was 'replaced' by Cleo Laine, who treated what was a highly sophisticated European blend of many musical elements as if it had been a jazz score by her husband. The result was regrettable, but not as regrettable as the events on the stage. Just as Sir Cecil Beaton is said to have referred to Puccini's *Turandot* as 'my *Chu Chin Chow*', Macmillan clearly conceived *The Seven Deadly Sins* as a debauched German counterpart of Sandy Wilson's *The Boy Friend*.

Much Anglo-Saxon reaction to the Brecht-Weill works is based on a misunderstanding. There is no doubt that some, possibly much, of the attraction of *The Seven Deadly Sins* (as

---

* Janet Flanner (Genêt): *Paris was Yesterday (1925–1939)*, New York and London, 1972/3. But the intended irony is based on a mistranslation.

well as *The Threepenny Opera* and *Mahagonny*) is the powerful scent of Weimar Republic decadence each gives off. This really clouds the issue. Weill was never a witty purveyor of chic decadence. But one would never suspect it after seeing a typical English production of his work. English productions of Weill (the Sadler's Wells *Mahagonny* was an honourable exception) are apt to place his works firmly in Sally Bowles country, with Mr Norris busily changing trains in the background. Yet the true decadence was in the society on which Brecht and Weill cast so cold and piercing an eye: not in their creations. Both *Mahagonny* and *The Seven Deadly Sins* are fiercely moral works. They are meant to shock and appal as well as amuse. They are attacks on what Brecht—and to some extent Weill—saw as the evils of a type of society which was fundamentally wrong. One does not have to go all the way with Brecht's analysis of the evils of capitalism to appreciate the fervour and conviction of his attack upon what a British Prime Minister has called its 'unacceptable face'. Thus to stigmatise these works as 'nasty' (as the late Dyneley Hussey once did) is as wrong-headed as to regard them as 'amusing'. They are neither: they are morality plays.

Given the power of works such as these, it is hard to see Weill's later career as anything but a tragedy. Consider, however, his position in the early 1930s. The country in which he had lived for thirty-three years, and in which his successes had been scored, was now closed to him. He was homeless. After the disappearance of *The Seven Deadly Sins* with the company that had created it, he tried other enterprises in Paris and in London. None succeeded. He set great score by his *Symphony No. 2*, written in 1933–4. It was given by a first-rate orchestra— the Concertgebouw—under an excellent conductor—Bruno Walter—in October, 1934, and torn to pieces by the critics, whose general tone implied that it was an impertinence for a mere theatre composer to venture into the concert hall with a symphony. Walter gave the work again three years later in Vienna, but the damage was done and the *Symphony* was not even printed until sixteen years after its composer had died. The musical world in general was hostile to Weill, in some cases virulently so. After hanging on in Europe for a couple of years, he left for America.

No one was interested in his symphonic work, and there was no market for works such as *Mahagonny* in the U.S. Weill was a professional to his fingertips: he was versatile, he could write melodies which remained in the memory, he knew how to score for a theatre orchestra and avoid the extravagances which caused *Porgy and Bess* to be withdrawn on economic grounds when it was still doing excellent business. In a word, he knew all the tricks of the trade. He turned his hand to musicals, to such purpose that there was no question of his having to live and die in straitened circumstances, like poor Bartók.

It is impossible not to admire the versatility with which Weill turned himself into one of the half-dozen or so most successful and most highly regarded composers of musicals in his adopted country, a name to stand beside those of Rodgers and Hart, Cole Porter, Gershwin, Harold Arlen. When and if the memoirs of Lotte Lenya appear, they may cast some light on what seems to have been a total abandonment by Weill of more 'serious' ventures. But, had he written them, who, in his lifetime, would have performed them? And Weill was not an Ives, a Charles Koechlin or a Havergal Brian, content to compose vast works which might never see the light of day. Weill was a working German theatre musician, used to conceiving his works in practical terms and used to getting them performed.

But the Broadway public was neither as sophisticated musically nor as alert mentally as the Germans for whom Weill had been accustomed to write; it was also politically much further to the right; and these factors had their effect on the music he wrote. So too did the temperament of the writers with whom he worked and the subject-matter with which he had to deal. This was nothing new: Weill-Brecht was very different from Weill-Kaiser. Now the asperities of Brecht were exchanged for the vaguely philanthropic yearnings of Maxwell Anderson or the slickness of Ira Gershwin, to name two of Weill's American collaborators. The bite disappeared from Weill's music, though the nostalgia remained, as in the famous *September Song*, which, though associated with the 1938 show *Knickerbocker Holiday*, had been written well before. But unrelieved nostalgia palls. In abandoning the pungency of his earlier style Weill said goodbye to much of its distinctive quality. His music often lacked character, though technically there was still much in it for more 'serious' composers to learn: his economical scoring, for instance, or the skill with which he wrote for Gertrude Lawrence's extremely limited voice in *Lady in the Dark*.

His American works divide naturally into two groups: 'serious' musicals, like *Knickerbocker Holiday*, *Street Scene* and *Lost in the Stars*, and lighter pieces, such as *Lady in the Dark* and *One Touch of Venus*, which contained the beautiful number *Speak Low*. There was also a Franz Werfel pageant, *The Eternal Road*, a play with music, *Johnny Johnson* (more like his early style but, significantly, written for a minority audience) and the student opera *Down in the Valley*. The first group in their various ways are all attempts at the Great American Musical (or even the Great American Opera). They all lack literary distinction and musical character; none of them has half the vigour of *Regina*. *Down in the Valley* is an unmitigated disaster. It was the lowest Weill ever sank. This 'pastoral' piece breathes Hollywood: it has none of the clear candour of Copland or Thomson. It bathes in easy sentiment and even introduces an angelic choir. It is all too easy to see why it became so popular at one time. It is amusing to spot among all the conscientious Americana one or two musical phrases that recall Weill's earlier manner: it is as if Mackie Messer or Widow Begbick had appeared for a moment to frighten the folksy characters out of their feeble wits.

Conclusion

Apart from the Second Viennese School, whose works I have excluded from this study for reasons already given, there are a number of other composers whose works do not fall into any of the categories so far considered but whose contribution to the music of the 1920s should be noted.

The music that Serge Prokofiev wrote at this time is among his best. It included three ballets for Diaghilev. The first, *Chout*, was first given at the Gâité-Lyrique in Paris with sets by Larionov and choreography by Larionov and Thadée Slavinsky, on 17 May, 1921. It was a grotesque story of Russian peasant life, whose strong feeling of nostalgia for the composer's native country was expressed not in the romantic manner of Rachmaninoff but tartly and crisply. On 7 June, 1927, Diaghilev presented at the Théâtre Sarah Bernhardt a second Prokofiev ballet, *Le Pas d'acier* ('The Dance of Steel'), choreographed by Massine and with constructivist sets after designs which the Soviet artist Yakoulov had made in Russia some years before. Diaghilev had already courted the disapproval of his rich patrons by having a Red Flag carried on stage during the final section of *L'Oiseau de feu*. Now he presented them with a fully-fledged Soviet ballet, and got away with it. Prokofiev's music was satisfactory, but has not lived.

His final ballet for Diaghilev was, unlike the previous two, a musical and balletic masterpiece. This was *Le Fils prodigue*, first seen at the Théâtre Sarah Bernhardt on 12 May, 1929, with choreography by Balanchine and sets and costumes by Georges Rouault. Serge Lifar danced the Prodigal Son, Felia Doubrovska the Siren, Michael Fedorov the Prodigal's Father, Leon Woizikovsky and Anton Dolin his friends.

The idea for the ballet had come, like so many excellent ideas for ballets, from Boris Kochno. Balanchine had been reminded of an episode in *The Stationmaster*, the short story by Pushkin. This describes a wayside inn at which travellers rest and change horses. The walls of the waiting-room are covered with primitive Russian pictures showing the story of the Prodigal Son. The last of the pictures shows the boy returning home, dragging himself along on his knees. This image inspired the final scene of the ballet, originally interpreted, very movingly, by Lifar, and since by Francisco Moncion, Edward Villella, and, unforgettably, by Hugh Laing, during the brief period in the early 1950s when he and Nora Kaye worked with the New York City Ballet.

For this ballet Prokofiev wrote a score which displays him at his finest. It later formed the basis of his *Fourth Symphony*, but it was more satisfactory in its original balletic form. It has its moments of clashing Prokofievian violence—notably in the dance for the two companions of the Prodigal Son—but its most striking and surprising feature is the simplicity and lyricism of its calmer movements, such as the first, *The Departure*, and the last sequence, *Awakening and Remorse* and *The Return Home*. Here Prokofiev pares down his earlier exuberance and is content with a clarity and reliance on melody that tell far more than elaboration and dissonant violence could ever do. Prokofiev could well afford to rely on melody, being one of the few twentieth-century masters with a natural and unforced gift in that direction. The result was a work which Prokofiev was seldom to match again: in his stage music only, perhaps, with the ballet *Romeo and Juliet*, that triumphant and almost unique rejoinder to the allegation that no composer of this century has the melodic power to sustain a three-act ballet.

Happily, *Le Fils prodigue* can still be seen. Balanchine revived it for his New York City Ballet, and it has also been taken into the repertory of the Royal Ballet, who give a creditable performance, even if, as usual, the essentials of the Balanchine style elude them. Rouault's sets are superb. To compare this work with, say, the *Job* of Vaughan Williams, Ninette de Valois and John Piper, is to highlight in one striking example the difference between the superb professionalism of three international masters working in concert and the worthy provincialism of three local talents.

Henri Sauguet has already been mentioned. Born in 1901 at Bordeaux, Sauguet was introduced to Diaghilev by Satie in Paris in 1924. Diaghilev wanted to meet the young man, whose piano pieces, the *Françaises*, he had heard played by Marcelle Meyer. But it was three years before Sauguet had a ballet produced by the Diaghilev Company: this was *La Chatte*, first performed at Monte Carlo on 30 April, 1927.

La Chatte was extremely successful at the time, though it made little money for its composer. According to Janet Flanner, all he got for it was 5,000 francs from Diaghilev, less than 1,000 from the publisher, another 700 or 800 every time the ballet was danced in France, and a mere 75 each time it was danced in England. Composers derived prestige from having a score accepted by Diaghilev, but they did not make their fortunes that way—though as a result of the prestige gained they stood a better chance of getting their work performed elsewhere. *La Chatte* had Balanchine choreography and sets and costumes by Gabo and Pevsner. The idea for the ballet came from Kochno (under the pseudonym of Sobeka), and the principal roles were danced by Olga Spessivtseva (later replaced by Nikitina and Markova) and Serge Lifar. It was really Lifar's ballet. Lightly clad for the period, he was carried round the stage in triumph by other personable young men and the effect created a sensation. Marc-César Scotto (p. 17) conducted the first performance; Desormière took over in Paris.

It was a pretty silly idea for a ballet. A young man falls in love with a cat. Through the power of Aphrodite the beast is transmuted into human form. Alas, during the lovemaking of the young man and the cat-woman, a mouse appears. This is too much for the heroine, who departs in pursuit and regains her animal shape. The idea was echoed in a much later ballet, *Les Demoiselles de la nuit*, which is also about a transformed cat's animal instincts triumphing over her love for a young man. This was the ballet in which Margot Fonteyn scored a great success with the Paris audience in the role of the cat Agathe. It was first given by the Ballets de Paris at the Théâtre Marigny in May, 1948. Based on an idea by Jean Anouilh, it had choreography by Roland Petit, music by Jean Françaix and sets and costumes by the cat-obsessed painter Léonor Fini.

Sauguet's score for *La Chatte* is charming though little more. Both in lyrical moments and more animated ones (such as the engaging *Jeux des garçons*) it suggests a latter-day Gounod.

Apparently he found the subject a very sympathetic one, being a lover of cats and the owner when young of a beast called Colonel Cody.

Another of Sauguet's many ballets was *La Nuit*, again from an idea by Kochno, this time with sets by Christian Bérard. It was first danced as part of C. B. Cochran's 1930 Revue at the Palace Theatre, Manchester, on 4 March, 1930. It is odd to think that the most sophisticated theatrical designer of the twentieth century made his debut at Manchester. Basically the story of a poor boy who meets a rich girl, only to have a symbolic stone wall rise to separate them, it was revived as a tribute to the recently dead Bérard by the Ballets des Champs-Elysées in April 1949, with new choreography by Janine Charrat. Sauguet's *La Rencontre*, on the story of Oedipus and the Sphinx (8 November, 1948, with sets by Bérard and choreography by David Lichine) is one of his best ballet scores. Dedicated to Kochno and Bérard, it conveys the sinister atmosphere of the encounter to perfection.

Satie influenced Sauguet strongly. This shows in the cantata *La Voyante* (1932), described as a *scène pour voix de femmes et petit orchestre* on words by Nostradamus. In the three movements, *Cartomancie*, *Astrologie* and *Chiromancie*, Sauguet follows Satie's structural procedures and the result is an agreeable work. But there is no echo, here or elsewhere in Sauguet's work, of the powerful effect which Satie could obtain from the simplest ingredients: it is charm all the way, though not to be despised for that.

The playwright Jean Anouilh, we have seen, provided the idea for *Les Demoiselles de la nuit*. Both Diaghilev and Rolf de Maré went to writers of consequence for ideas for ballets. This concept of the poet or the writer as *auteur* of a ballet is more or less peculiar to France, and the tradition has been continued. Jacques Prévert provided the idea for *Le Rendez-vous* (Kosma–Petit–Picasso–Brassaï–Mayo); Louise de Vilmorin for *La Perle* (Pascal–Gsovsky–Zao-Wou-Ki); Anouilh for the strange and compelling ballet *Le Loup* (Dutilleux–Petit–Carzou); Orson Welles for *The Lady in the Ice* (Damase–Petit–Welles); Simenon for *La Chambre* (Auric–Petit–Buffet). In his *Journal du voleur* Jean Genet refers to the conception of his ballet *'adame Miroir*, with sets by the Belgian surrealist Paul Delvaux. The piece was concerned, to no one's surprise, with sailors and death.

Where ballet was concerned, the spirit of the 1920s did not long survive in a direct way. The companies of Colonel de Basil and of René Blum could not match the artistic excitement of the Diaghilev Company and the Swedish Ballet, though they possessed superb dancers and had much to offer. The Diaghilev spirit made a brief but brilliant reappearance four years after the Russian impresario's death with the *Ballets 1933*, which gave a number of performances that year in Paris and London. The enterprise sprang from the desire of the rich Englishman Edward James to provide a company of which his wife, Tilly Losch, could be the star. Balanchine was hired as choreographer and Kochno as artistic director. Apart from Losch, the company was led by the very young Tamara Toumanova, Roman Jasinsky, Nathalie Leslie (later Krassovska) and, in London only, the beautiful Pearl Argyle.

The company had a repertoire of six ballets, for all of which Balanchine provided the choreography. Apart from *The Seven Deadly Sins*, already discussed (pp. 115–121), these were *Fastes*, on a scenario by André Derain about a pagan festival in ancient Italy (music by Sauguet and sets by Derain himself); *Les Songes*, with music by Milhaud and designs again by Derain; *Les Valses de Beethoven*, with music arranged by Nabokov and sets by Emilio Terry; *Errante*, with music arranged by Charles Koechlin from Schubert's 'Wanderer' Fantasia and very remarkable sets by Tchelitchew; and *Mozartiana* to Tchaikovsky's *Fourth Suite*, with designs by Bérard. For the London season, at the Savoy, the company alternated with the *Ballets Serge Lifar*, also presented by James, but led by Lifar and Nikitina and presenting a separate repertory. But James was not content merely to present ballets. In Paris there were performances during the season of *Job*, an oratorio by Nicolas Nabokov for baritone, tenor, male chorus and orchestra, which was presented as part of the ballet programme without dancing but with projections of engravings from a sixteenth-century English Bible. In London he was even more ambitious, as will be seen.

James was an admirer of the Neo-Romantic or Neo-Humanist group of painters, whose first exhibition had been at the Galerie Druet in Paris in February 1926. Those who exhibited on that occasion were Tchelitchew, Bérard, Eugène Berman, Berman's brother Léonid, and Kristians Tonny. The first two of these were given the opportunity to design sets for the ballet season, and there was intense rivalry between Tchelitchew and Bérard, each of whom had his supporters among the Parisian public.

Though the official first night in London was on 30 June, James elected to open with a *répétition générale* (unusual in London, then as now) with an entirely invited audience, on 28 June. The programme for the occasion was *Anna-Anna*, conducted by Maurice de Abravanel, followed by *Mozartiana* and *Errante*, both conducted by Constant Lambert. In an earlier book* I wrongly stated that Lambert, who much admired *Anna-Anna* (*The Seven Deadly Sins*) conducted it during the London season alternately with Abravanel. In fact Abravanel (naturally enough, as a composition pupil of Weill's) was in charge of *The Seven Deadly Sins* at all its performances, though, of course, Lambert gained during the season the chance to familiarise himself with the work.

The London season closed on 18 July not with a ballet performance but with a concert in the Savoy Theatre. This began with the *Kleine Dreigroschenmusik* (Weill's suite from *The Threepenny Opera*) and continued with a performance of Igor Markevitch's *Les Hymnes* under Lambert. There followed Milhaud's *Sur la mort d'un tyran*, a curious work for chorus, piccolo, clarinet, tuba and percussion on a text by the Roman historiographer Lampridius, in a French translation by Diderot. This is concerned with the rejoicing of the Roman populace at the death of the tyrannical Emperor Commodus. The chorus is called upon to shout and speak together as well as to sing. In some ways the work curiously anticipates the off-stage shouts of 'Death to the Etruscans' during that odd Child's Guide to Roman History provided by the Male and Female Chorus in the original version of Britten's *Rape of Lucretia*. It is worth recalling that Milhaud's *Pan et Syrinx* was not without its influence on Britten's *Les Illuminations*.

As if all this were not enough for the London audience, Lotte Lenya (who had earlier been reported indisposed)

* *Constant Lambert*, London, 1973.

appeared at 11 p.m. to sing in *Mahagonny*. I have been unable to establish whether the work performed was *Das kleine Mahagonny* or selections from the full-length opera. I imagine the latter; at all events the complete work could hardly have been given. The press the following day seemed stunned by the whole event, as well they might have been, particularly as *Mahagonny*, being heard in London for the first time, was described in the programme as comparable to Mozart or to 'Cole Porter at his best moments'. Like *The Seven Deadly Sins*, it was seen as a sordid story of American low life, though some critics expressed gratitude at hearing at last a work which had created such a furore on the Continent.

Mr James's enterprise displayed an artistic boldness fully worthy of Diaghilev; but his company was soon disbanded.

What was to become of the musical talents of the 1920s? We have already seen how Hindemith, Křenek and Weill changed, none, alas, for the better. The minor figure of Vladimir Dukelsky developed in a way not dissimilar to Weill. He had written for Diaghilev in 1925 the ballet *Zéphire et Flore*, an attempt to reproduce in modern terms the type of mythological ballet danced by the private companies of Russian nobles at the time of Tsar Alexander I. It had been Kochno's idea. Braque designed it, and the young Oliver Messel provided 'masks and symbols' (it was his first work for the theatre). Dukelsky followed his 'serious' style for a time, writing the ballet *Jardin public* on an idea from Gide's novel *Les Faux-monnayeurs* for de Basil in 1935, but eventually he changed his professional name to Vernon Duke and became an avowedly popular composer, in which role he enjoyed considerable success with songs like *April in Paris* and shows like *Cabin in the Sky*. Nabokov continued to compose in much the same style as his music of the 1920s, contributing a piece of mock-Americana to the de Basil repertory in the form of the once-popular ballet *Union Pacific*. He finally found his role as UNESCO pundit, author and raconteur. Like Dukelsky and Nabokov, Rieti also went to live in the U.S., where he continued to write music of some distinction, notably the ballet-cantata *The Triumph of Bacchus and Ariadne* (p. 88) and the cantata *Ulysses* on words by Edward James (1939).

In Britain Berners pursued his own way without significant

change of style, and Lambert's roots remained in the 1920s, when he had made his name. William Walton, on the other hand, grew maturer, or, perhaps, duller. There is little in his later work—apart from *Belshazzar's Feast*—to match the animation and style of such early works as *Façade* (1926), too well known to need description, or the *Sinfonia Concertante* of 1928 for orchestra with piano, which had originally been conceived as a ballet but had been rejected by Diaghilev.

The neoclassicism to which Stravinsky had adhered in the 1920s grew blander, and, in the end, of course, he adopted a serial style, albeit of a very individual nature. Of the *Six*, Milhaud's work began in general to decline in quality and increase in quantity, while Auric's revealed more clearly that vein of romanticism only hinted at in the 1920s.

Poulenc's development offered no surprises, though it proved most fruitful. His style, perhaps, deepened, but it did not reveal totally new qualities—merely developments of qualities already present or at least adumbrated in the music he had written in the 1920s. Personal setbacks and increasing age caused his religious side to be shown more overtly, but it had been present in his personality from the beginning.

Nothing, though, could have been more '1920ish' than the *Concerto for two pianos and orchestra*, written in 1932 to a commission from the Princesse Edmond de Polignac and first played at Venice on 5 September, 1932, during that year's Festival of the International Society for Contemporary Music, by the composer and Jacques Février, under the baton of Désiré Defauw. The opening *Allegro ma non troppo* and the final *Allegro molto* show Poulenc at his most Parisian and frivolous, while the *Larghetto* that comes between displays his charming lyrical vein. There is an amusing anecdote about this work. Poulenc was in Amsterdam to appear as soloist in it with the Concertgebouw Orchestra under Otto Klemperer, not an obvious conductor for the piece. Klemperer grew increasingly irritated both by the music and by the composer's habit of absenting himself from rehearsals, tempted, no doubt, by some aspects of the life of that most easygoing of cities. The climax came when Klemperer, incensed by the personality of the composer and the 'triviality' of his music, leaned over to the leader of the orchestra and inquired *Was ist Französisch für Scheiss?*

Two later works of Poulenc, both deriving clearly from the 1920s, represent the composer at his best and—despite the apparent 'frivolity' of the second—his most serious. The first of these is the cantata with orchestra, or choral suite, *Sécheresses*, written in 1937 and first performed at the Concerts Colonne the following year under Paul Paray. This work, as David Drew has pointed out, is a translation into words and music of the surrealist aesthetic which flourished after the 1914–18 War. It is the world of Salvador Dali and Yves Tanguy. The poems are by Edward James once again, himself a notable collector of surrealist canvases. They describe a world which has been deprived of all life and all vegetation by the ravages of the sun and the lack of rain. They suggest the parched surrealist landscapes which can be seen in our museums. The four movements are *Les Sauterelles* ('The Grasshoppers'), *Le Village abandonné*, *Le Faux Avenir* and *La Squelette de la mer*. The last describes the last living creature, a shellfish, only just able to stir itself slightly among the surrounding desolation. Poulenc achieves his effects without violence and without overbearing dissonance: the very blandness of the music reinforces its sinister atmosphere. Though the composer had considerable doubts about the work, it is one of his best.

The second work is a very different affair. The 1939–45 War had, naturally, a deep effect on Poulenc. It led him, for one thing, to reaffirm his love for all things French in his third ballet, *Les Animaux modèles*. The work, based on the *Fables* of La Fontaine, was set by the painter Maurice Brianchon in a little Burgundian town in the seventeenth century. The music has an ineffable tenderness and warmth. In *Les Mamelles de Tirésias*, by contrast, the inspiration was very different. This *opéra-bouffe* in a prologue and two acts used as its text Guillaume Apollinaire's surrealist play which ironically urged Frenchmen and Frenchwomen to *faire des enfants*. Like *Sécheresses*, the opera is a masterpiece, but a very odd one, made up of parody after parody and veering inconsequently from the wildest knockabout humour to deeply-felt lyricism. Written in 1944, it was not seen until 1947, when Albert Wolff conducted the first performance (3 June) at the Opéra-Comique, with designs by Erté and Denise Duval in the female lead.

A number of younger composers responded to the aesthetic

of the 1920s. In France Jean Françaix continued the tradition, as, after the 1939–45 War, did Jean-Michel Damase, born in 1928, who had been the pianist at the *Soirées de la danse* in Paris in 1944 out of which the Ballets des Champs–Elysées were born. Damase's *ballet avec chansons, La Croqueuse de diamants* (theme by Roland Petit and Alfred Adam, lyrics by the poet Raymond Queneau, designs by Wakhevitch) was, in its way, a very 1920ish concept. Renée Jeanmaire took the lead at the performances in Paris and New York in 1950. Joseph Kosma, writer of songs and film music and a committed left-winger, owed more than a little to Weill. In England, Walter Leigh, a Hindemith pupil, wrote a neoclassic *Harpsichord Concertino* and some incidental music in the music-hall manner for *The Frogs* of Aristophanes, as well as a commercially very successful comic opera, *Jolly Roger*. Leigh had great talent, but unhappily he was killed in action in the Western Desert during the last war.

But it was perhaps among American composers as much as anywhere that the spirit of the 1920s survived. Virgil Thomson, for instance, born in Kansas City in 1896, spent the years 1921–2 and 1925–32 in Paris, and the musical climate of the city had an indelible influence on him, one which mingled with his love of Southern hymnody and American folk song. His *Capital, Capitals* (1927) for four male voices and piano, on words by Gertrude Stein, is a hilarious work. The following year he finished his opera *Four Saints in Three Acts*, again on words by Miss Stein, which had to wait until February 1934 for its first staged performance, at Hartford, Connecticut, by a group with an attractive name: the Society of Friends and Enemies of Modern Music. Alexander Smallens conducted a performance in which all the parts—the leading ones being the Spanish saints Teresa and Ignatius—were taken by a black cast; the sets were by Florine Stettheimer, the choreography by Frederick Ashton. It must surely have been one of the campest spectacles to grace any stage, and one's only regret is that Ronald Firbank was not alive to see it. The music has great lyrical charm, as have many of Thomson's later works, which have not departed significantly from his earlier style.

Paul Bowles, better known, at least in Britain, as an accom-

plished novelist, has written equally accomplished works
which reveal the influences of Stravinsky, Poulenc and the
'Castilian' Falla, as well as the music of Morocco, where
Bowles lived for so long. In style if not in date his *Picnic Cantata*
is very much of the 1920s, as is the *Music for a Farce*, based on
incidental music Bowles wrote for a projected production of
the William Gillette farce *Too much Johnson* at the Mercury
Theater, New York, in 1938.

Finally, there is Ned Rorem, hardly known at all in Britain,
which is unfortunate, since he is one of the finest song composers alive today. Born in 1923, Rorem to some degree
repeated the Parisian experience of his mentor, Virgil Thomson.
In the early 1950s he came to Paris, armed with all the right
introductions and blessed not only with considerable talent
but with remarkable good looks. Rorem's account of these
years makes fascinating reading. He is a name-dropper and
a narcissist, but he has some excellent names to drop and he is
a narcissist with a knowledge of his own narcissism. The
photographs in the book* show Rorem with Marie-Laure de
Noailles, Rorem with Thomson, Rorem with Auric, with
Copland, with Julius Katchen, with Kochno, with Julien
Green, with the Barraults; they also show Rorem by Cocteau,
by Cartier-Bresson, by Man Ray, by Carl van Vechten.
Rorem, naturally, attended the ball given in Venice in 1951
(the year of the premiere there of *The Rake's Progress*) by
Carlos de Beistegui, in its way an apotheosis of those lavish
entertainments given in the Paris of the 1920s by the Beau-
monts and the Noailles. Rorem's music, too, harks back,
though in an individual way, to the 1920s. His *Eleven Studies
for Eleven Players*, written in response to a Buffalo University
commission in 1959, display a deftness, wit and economy of
effect quite outstanding in a composer of our day, as well as a
vein of tender lyricism almost as unusual. Through Thomson
and through his Parisian friends, Rorem traces his ancestry
back to the 1920s.

But in general the composers of today follow a very different
aesthetic. The 1920s can now be seen as a period that is over,
their aesthetic as one which has little influence left. To
summarise the achievements of the decade is an impossible

* *The Paris Diary of Ned Rorem.*

task. Apart from the works we have discussed, the 1920s saw the appearance of such masterpieces as Puccini's *Turandot*, Berg's *Wozzeck*, Szymanowski's *Le Roi Roger*, Fauré's *Second Piano Quintet* and his song cycle *L'Horizon chimérique*. It produced personal statements like Ravel's *L'Enfant et les sortilèges* and universal works like *Les Noces*. To me the spirit of the 1920s in music is to be heard at its best and its most typical in Satie's *Parade* and *Socrate;* Poulenc's *Les Biches, Aubade* and *Sécheresses;* Weill's *Mahagonny* and *The Seven Deadly Sins;* Stravinsky's *Pulcinella;* Milhaud's *La Création du monde;* Lambert's *Piano Concerto* and *The Rio Grande.* This is a personal choice: there are plenty of other works that could stand beside those I have listed. If one has to choose only one voice, it must, I think, be that of Kurt Weill, who, more than any other figure, speaks with the authentic and unforgettable accents of the time, its cynicism, its pessimism, its bravery, and its gaiety that contains more than a hint of despair.

Discography

These notes are selective. They do not by any means cover all the works mentioned during the course of the book, many of which in any case remain unrecorded. Where there is a profusion of recordings (as in the cases of Stravinsky and Satie) I have confined myself to the briefest of pointers. I have, however, mentioned deleted recordings (D) when they are of special interest or merit, might still be found, or might deserve reissue. All recordings are in stereo unless otherwise stated. The arrangement is alphabetical by names of composers.

AURIC, Georges (see also SIX, LES)

Auric has not been well served by the record companies. Only one work of consequence is currently available on disc, and that in a special edition. This is *Les Fâcheux*, available in France (and in specialist shops in the U.K.) in a two-disc album by the Orchestra of the Monte Carlo Opera under Igor Markevitch: Guilde Internationale du Disque SMS 5227–8. The album also contains *Les Biches* by Poulenc (complete), *La Chatte* by Sauguet, *Le Train bleu* by Milhaud (cut), and *Jack in the Box* by Satie. Recording and performance are both adequate, and it could be argued that the sound of a good French theatre orchestra is more appropriate to these works than the super-smoothness of, say, the Berlin Philharmonic. In any case four of the five works are rarities, so that one cannot pick and choose.

Phèdre was once available in mono as part of another two-disc album, by the Paris Conservatoire Orchestra under Georges Tzipine: Columbia 33CX 1252–3 (U.K.), Angel 35117–8 (U.S.). The album, called *La Groupe des Six*, contained works by all the composers of the Group. The performances were good and idiomatic.

BERNERS, Lord

The suite from *Triumph of Neptune* is available in the U.K. in a mono recording by the Philadelphia Orchestra under

Beecham: CBS 61431. The performance was recorded around 1950 and is good, except that in the *Schottische* members of the Orchestra emit would-be 'Scottish' yells. These are not in the score and do not help.

BLITZSTEIN, Marc

Regina has never been available in the U.K. but was till recently available in the U.S. as a three-disc album by the New York City Opera under Krachmalnick: Columbia 03S 202. Performance and recording are excellent.

BLOCH, Ernest

The *Concerto Grosso* No. 1 is available in the U.S. in two different performances: Mercury 75017 and Everest 3328.

CASELLA, Alfredo

The ballet *La Giara* is available in the U.S. It is played by the St Cecilia Orchestra under Previtali: London STS-15024.

DEBUSSY, Claude-Achille

Le Martyre de Saint-Sébastien has nothing to do with the 1920s but has been discussed during the book in connection with Ida Rubinstein. Only one recording of the work is available in the U.K.: Decca SDD 314, under Ansermet. This is without any spoken text. The recording is twenty years old and the performance lacklustre. Munch's performance, available in the U.S. (RCA VICS-1404) is much better, but again oldish, and marred by some fruity recitation by the conductor himself. Ormandy's performance (D) with Zorina, Hilda Gueden and the Philadelphia Orchestra was better than either: CBS SBRG 72078–9 (U.K.), MS 6107–8 (U.S.). This contains the essential part of the text, with some cuts. The most authentic and stylistically perfect performance ever recorded was by the Orchestre du Théâtre des Champs-Elysées and various other artists under Inghelbrecht: Ducretet Thomson DTL 93040–1 (mono, D). The Orchestra was far from virtuoso and the recording by present-day standards antediluvian: but the style is absolutely right.

FALLA, Manuel de
All the works mentioned in the book have been well recorded in versions still available in both the U.S. and the U.K.

FRANÇAIX, Jean
The *Piano Concertino* is available in the U.K. but not apparently in the U.S. in a good performance, well recorded by Claude Françaix and the London Symphony Orchestra under Dorati: Philips SAL 3637. The disc also contains Satie's *Parade* and Milhaud's *Le Boeuf sur le Toit*.

HINDEMITH, Paul
Hin und Zurück is available in a performance by the Berlin Symphony Orchestra under Grüber: Vox STGBY 662 (U.K.), Candide 31044 (U.S.)

HONEGGER, Arthur (see also SIX, LES)
The Prelude, Fugue and Postlude from *Amphion* were once available on the album *La Groupe des Six* (mono: see Auric). Good performance.
Jeanne d'Arc au bûcher is not currently available in the U.S. It is available in the U.K. in a performance by the London Symphony Chorus and Orchestra under Ozawa: CBS 77216. *Le Roi David* is available in three different performances in the U.K. and two in the U.S. Particularly interesting is Charles Dutoit's recording of the original version: Erato STU 70667–8 (U.K. only).
Pacific 231 has been much recorded.

KÜNNEKE, Eduard
The *Tänzerische Suite* was once available in Germany only in a historic recording, made in 1938, by the Berlin Philharmonic Orchestra under the composer: Telefunken HT 13 (mono).

MILHAUD, Darius (see also SIX, LES)
Le Boeuf sur le Toit is available in the U.K. under Dorati (see Françaix) and in the U.S. under the composer: Nonesuch 71122. Golschmann, the original conductor, once recorded it on Capitol P 8244 (mono).
Le Carnaval d'Aix derives from *Salade*. Available in both U.S.

and U.K. under the composer: Candide 31013 (U.S.), Vox STGBY 640 (U.K.)

Le Carnaval de Londres has been recorded in Russia, of all places, by the Chamber Ensemble of the Leningrad Philharmonic under Fedotov: Melodiya 33C 01473–74 (a). Performance and recording are bright and good. The disc also contains a suite from *Barabau* by Rieti.

La Création du monde has been much recorded.

L'Homme et son désir is available under the composer: Candide 31008 (U.S.), Vox STGBY 626 (U.K.)

Le Pauvre Matelot is regrettably unavailable. There was a mono recording in the chamber version under the composer on Vega C30 A69. The recorded quality was poor, the performance good, apart from a shrill performance of the heroine by Jacqueline Brumaire.

Salade—see *Le Carnaval d'Aix*.

Scaramouche has been much recorded.

Le Train bleu, somewhat cut, is available coupled with *Les Fâcheux* and other works (see Auric).

PIERNÉ, Gabriel

Cydalise et le chèvre-pied and the *Divertissements sur un thème pastoral* are available with the *Concertstück* in France on Erato STU 70587. The performance under Martinon and the recording are both excellent.

POULENC, Francis (see also SIX, LES)

Les Animaux modèles (suite only) is available: HMV ASD 2316 (U.K.), Angel S-36421 (U.S.). The performance is by the Paris Conservatoire Orchestra under Georges Prêtre.

The *Aubade* is available in three performances in the U.S. only. The best is Gabriel Tacchino's (Angel S-36426). It is not, however, the equal of Poulenc's own (deleted): Vega C30 ST 20006.

Le Bal masqué is not currently available. Pierre Bernac recorded it with Poulenc at the piano and a group of players under Louis Frémaux (mono, D): Westminster XWN 18422 (U.S.)

The suite from *Les Biches* is obtainable in the U.S. under Prêtre (Angel S-35932) and in the U.K. under Frémaux (HMV ASD 2989). This suite is composed of five movements: *Rondeau, Adagietto, Rag-Mazurka, Andantino, Finale*. When Desormière recorded a suite (Decca LXT 2720, and later ACL 189, both D) he also included the first *Chanson dansée*, without chorus. *Les Biches* is also available complete, with chorus (see Auric) on SMS 5227–8.

The best recording of the *Concert champêtre* is probably that by Aimée van de Wiele with the Paris Conservatoire Orchestra under Prêtre: HMV ASD 517 (U.K.), Angel S-35993 (U.S.) It is conveniently coupled with the *Concerto for Two Pianos and Orchestra*, played by Poulenc and Jacques Février, of which there are also alternative performances available in both U.S. and U.K.

The *Litanies à la Vierge noire de Rocamadour* have been recorded by the Choir of St John's College, Cambridge: Argo ZRG-662 (U.K. and U.S.)

Les Mamelles de Tirésias has been recorded only once, by a cast headed by Denise Duval and conducted by André Cluytens. The recording was last available on Seraphim 60029 (mono, D).

Sécheresses was once available in a good performance by the Chorale Elisabeth Brasseur and the Paris Conservatoire Orchestra under Tzipine (mono, D)—see Auric.

The *Suite française* is obtainable in the U.S. under Prêtre: Angel S-36519.

There are various recordings of the *Trio*, notably one by members of the Melos Ensemble: Angel S-36586 (U.S.), HMV ASD 2506 (U.K.) Poulenc recorded it on Vega C35 A 181 (mono, D).

PROKOFIEV, Serge

The best recording of *Chout* (suite only) is by the London Symphony under Abbado: Decca SXL 6286 (U.K.), London 6522 (U.S.)

The only current recording of *Le Fils prodigue* is unsatisfactory. There was a good performance by the New York City Ballet Orchestra under Leon Barzin: Vox PL 9310 (mono, D), rather roughly recorded.

A suite from *Le Pas d'acier* has been recorded by the Moscow Radio Orchestra under Rozhdestvensky: Melodiya/Angel S-40017 (U.S.), HMV SLS 844 (U.K.)

RAVEL, Maurice

Gérard Souzay's recording of the *Chansons madécasses* (Philips 839733—U.S.) is by far the best. Janet Baker, though as beautiful vocally as ever, is unidiomatic; and the words suggest a male singer.

Where *L'Enfant et les sortilèges* is concerned, Ansermet's recording, though old (1955), is to be preferred to Maazel's. It is on Decca SDD 168 (U.K.), Richmond 33086 (U.S.) The two *Piano Concertos* are much recorded. Alicia de Larrocha's recent coupling on Decca SXL 6680 (U.K.) has been highly praised.

RIETI, Vittorio

A suite from *Barabau* has been recorded—see Milhaud: *Le Carnaval de Londres*.

ROREM, Ned

The *Eleven Studies for Eleven Players* are available in the U.S. on Louisville S-644.

SATIE, Erik

Satie has been very extensively recorded in recent years, but the quality of the performances has been extremely variable. Among performances of *Les Aventures de Mercure* is one on a two-disc set by the Utah Symphony under Abravanel which also includes, *inter alia*, performances of *En habit de cheval*, part of *La Belle Excentrique*, *Jack in the Box*, *Parade*, *Relâche*, the *Trois morceaux en forme de poire* and the *Cinq grimaces pour un songe d'une nuit d'été*: 2-Vanguard C-10037-8 (U.S.), Pye/Vanguard VCS 10037-8 (U.K.). It is a useful package but the performances are no more than serviceable. Among complete performances of *La Belle Excentrique* is one on a disc by the 'Die Reihe' Ensemble under Cerha and other artists which also contains, *inter alia*, performances of *Parade*, *Le Piège de Méduse* (suite only) and the *Entr'acte* from *Relâche*: Candide 31018 (U.S.), Vox Candide STGBY 646 (U.K.). The performances are no more than fair.

The best performances of *Parade* are that by the Paris Conservatoire Orchestra under Auriacombe (which also includes *Relâche*)—HMV ASD 2369 (U.K.), Angel S-36486

(U.S.); and that by the London Symphony under Dorati—
see Français.

For a performance of *Le Piège de Méduse* with Satie's text
(and Pierre Bertin participating) there is Angel S-36713
(U.S. only).

Much of Satie's piano music, including the *Sports et
divertissements*, the *Trois gnossiennes* and the *Trois gymnopédies*,
has been recorded several times.

It is not possible wholeheartedly to recommend any of the
currently available versions of *Socrate*. The best performance
ever recorded was by Anne Laloë and an orchestra under
Sauguet: Le Chant du Monde LDX-A 8.292 (French
mono, D).

SAUGUET, Henri

La Chatte is available in a good performance on SMS
5227–8—see Auric.

Les Forains has been well recorded by the Lamoureux
Orchestra under the composer: Le Chant du Monde
LDX-S 8.300 (French, D).

SIX, LES

Les Mariés de la Tour Eiffel is available in the U.K. in a
French recording by Pierre Bertin, Jacques Duby and the
French Radio Orchestra under Milhaud: Adès 15.501.
This is an historic recording, marred only by the omission
of Milhaud's fugue *La Massacre* and by the presence of a
tiresomely coy *speakerine*.

STRAVINSKY, Igor

Few of Stravinsky's works remain unrecorded in adequate
or more than adequate performances.

L'Histoire du soldat is very effective in suite form, but even
more so complete. There was a particularly good performance by Cocteau, Ustinov and instrumentalists under
Igor Markevitch: French Philips 835.181 LY (D).

Curiously, there has yet to be a completely satisfactory
recording of *Les Noces*. Stravinsky's own (CBS BRG 72071—
U.K., ML 5772—U.S., D) was not very good. Boulez'
(Nonesuch 71133—U.S.) made very uncomfortable listening
because of the very close balance.

Perséphone is not currently available at all. Stravinsky's own performance (ML 5196—U.S.) was very good, but marred by Vera Zorina's recitation.

The best recording of the complete *Pulcinella* is the composer's own: in 3-Col. D3S–761 (U.S.), and on CBS 72452 (U.K., now D).

THOMSON, Virgil

A shortened version of *Four Saints in Three Acts*, recorded under the composer in 1947, was available in mono on RCA Victor RB 6608 (U.K.) and LM 2756 (U.S.). It is now deleted.

The suite from *The Plow that Broke the Plains* is available in the U.S., played by the Symphony of the Air under Stokowski and coupled with the suite from *The River*, on Vanguard 2095.

WEILL, Kurt

Aufstieg und Fall der Stadt Mahagonny is available in the U.K. in a very fine performance under Wilhelm Brückner-Rüggeberg: CBS 77341, 3 discs. One's only reservation— as in all recordings by Lotte Lenya in the 1950s—is that because of her age and the condition of her voice a certain amount of transposition was necessary. Nor, in the *Crane Duet*, does it blend well with that of the Jimmy. But she is so much inside the style and atmosphere that this is a small price to pay. Gisela Litz is superb as Widow Begbick.

Die Dreigroschenoper has been much recorded. There is an excellent performance with a cast headed by Lenya and with Brückner-Rüggeberg as conductor currently available in the U.K. on CBS 78279 (2 discs). This also includes songs from *Das Berliner Requiem*, *Der Silbersee* and *Happy End*. *Happy End*, again with Lenya, has now been deleted in the U.K. but is still available in the U.S.: CSP COS-2032. *Die sieben Todsünden* is obtainable in a serviceable perform-ance by Gisela May in the U.S.: DG 139308. Lenya's performance on Philips A 07186 L (mono, D) was in a class of its own, though again transposed and not well recorded. The two *Symphonies* are coupled in two U.K. recordings: by the BBC Symphony Orchestra under Gary Bertini (Argo

ZRG 755) and by the Leipzig Gewandhaus Orchestra under Edo de Waart (Philips 6500 642).

Since the preparation of the above discography there have been several changes in the U.K. record catalogues. Five recordings have been deleted. These are *Hin und Zurück* by Hindemith, *Jeanne d'Arc au bûcher* by Honegger, *Les Animaux modèles* by Poulenc, Auriacombe's recording of Satie's *Parade* and the complete *Mahagonny*. Two deleted performances have been reissued: the Künneke *Tänzerische Suite* on Telefunken Dokumente AJ6 41906 and Weill's *Happy End* on CBS 73463. Finally, Poulenc's *Aubade* has been issued in a performance by Joela Jones with the London Symphony Orchestra under Paul Freeman on Ember/Pye ECL 9036.

Index

Musical works are listed under the names of their composers, literary works under the names of their authors.